THE POWER OF YIDDISH THINKING

THE
POWER
OF
YIDDISH
THINKING

by Martin Marcus

DOUBLEDAY & COMPANY, INC.
Garden City, New York
1971

Library of Congress Catalog Card Number 79-144280
Printed in the United States of America
First Edition

L'chaim—To life!

CONTENTS

"Who will be the Jews fifty years from now?"
—David Korengold

THE POWER OF YIDDISH THINKING

Right away I should admit there probably is no such thing as Yiddish Thinking. Only one out of ten people I asked believed in it. Four out of the ten just gave me a glazed look. Three socked me in the mouth, and two said they weren't sure but felt that President Nixon would solve it. The results were more or less the same when I then queried Gentiles. I was quick to surmise that in Yiddish Thinking I had my hands on the perfect subject, one that is imaginary and, hence, one on which the author can hardly be assailed for inaccuracy. At the same time, an imaginary subject which gets people to socking one another and looking glazed maybe needs to be invented.

To speak of the *power* of Yiddish Thinking, then, is really to put myself in the soup (chicken, naturally). If you were asked to recall the one thing in history Jews are least famous for, you would probably say power. Of course, Jews are not famous for many other things—including polo, naval science, Renaissance painting and bullfighting. But mostly Jews are not famous for power. And yet they ought to be.

The power of Yiddish Thinking is the ability to survive at

the emotional cliff edges of life. It is the private ego's last
line of defense against fanaticism, propaganda, vogues and
all other forms of mass bamboozlement. I don't suggest for
a minute that this prowess belongs to Jews alone. It is a
human ability, something like dieting, which only the most
devoted, or desperate, practice with success. The Jews, perhaps more than any other of history's folk, have been made to
feast at the table of fanaticism and bamboozlement. No
wonder they have become expert ideological weight-watch-
ers. Not all Jews, of course. In fact, today more and more
one finds Polish, Negro, Irish Catholic, or just-plain-vanilla-
gentile practitioners of Yiddish Thinking.

The balance of misery in the world is changing. The good
old minority groups no longer have exclusive claim to frustra-
tion and crap-taking. Scapegoats are multiplying like scape
rabbits. When for a zillion years, a white skin and not much
else made you some kind of a big shot, now suddenly lack of
melanin has become at least suspect. Short hair and regular
church attendance are vaguely disreputable. Conservative
clothing may mark you as a Yahoo, or worse, without soul,
as that word is defined today. Soon Rotary membership may
be considered downright subversive!

Add to all this the newfangled terrors of pollution, auto-
mation and public craziness which nag white and black, rich
and poor, commie fanatic and capitalist pig alike, and you
know what you have? You have what I call a *cockamehmeh*
world. And to cope with a *cockamehmeh* world, you need a
cockamehmeh thought process, whoever you may be. You need
the Power of Yiddish Thinking.

Well, then, who are the great Yiddsh Thinkers of history?
Baron Rothschild? Uh uh. Bernard Baruch? Hardly. Einstein?
Nah. One of the true greats was the late produce wholesaler
Harry Stein of Chicago, who once confidently remarked of a
television performer, "Such a gorgeous orange dress," al-

though he was watching a black-and-white set. As I recall, the inscrutable comment had the effect of throwing some noisy guests into a mystified silence, allowing Harry and myself to enjoy the remainder of a program worthy of strict attention.

Another fabulous Yiddish Thinker of our day is my absent-minded Aunt Zinnia, who, during a condolence call, once congratulated the widow! Before the assembled mourners could work up a good gasp, Aunt Zinnia had successfully attributed her social error to a confusing bus trip. Or my friend Morrie the innkeeper, who sought a grand name to put up in neon for his new motel. I gave him distinguished alternatives ranging from the Exeter Arms to the Royal Regency. He settled finally for the Rio.

"At a hundred dollars a letter," said Morrie, "it's a grand name."

There are thousands, probably millions of Harrys, Aunt Zinnias and Morries in the world. Little people who know something you and I and Einstein don't know about getting along in it. Oddly enough, they would probably be the last to acknowledge their skill as wielders of anything so fancy as the Power of Yiddish Thinking. They would read this book and say "Phooey! Common sense! Yiddish is a language, not a thinking!"* But even the Yiddish word for it refutes them. *Sechel* means more than common sense, more than native intelligence or conventional knowledge. *Sechel* is . . . well, it's . . . ah . . . The Power of Yiddish Thinking!

---

* You will find in this book a few Yiddish expressions without immediate explanation. It is not necessary to understand them in order to enjoy the book fully. Still, you'll check every once in a while the glossary, it wouldn't kill you.

1

THE BIG PUTDOWN
or
Who Needs Fishes?

First, let's quickly dispense with the notion that one must use Yiddish words to express Yiddish thoughts. Years ago a friend who happens to speak fluent Yiddish spent an afternoon viewing that elaborate outdoor fish menagerie near Miami known as the Seaquarium. There were marine animals of every description, all frolicking in their natural habitats. Wherever he walked, this friend was inundated with fish literature or lectured at by guides. The whole atmosphere at the place was one of reverence toward creatures of the sea. On leaving the grounds, my friend noticed a guest register. Tourists from all over the world had signed the book and inscribed such effusions as: "Fabulous!" "Fascinating!" "An amazing experience," and so on. He added his name to the list, and then, Thinking Yiddish, in the space reserved for comments he wrote simply, "Vot is?"

Unquestionably, the heart and soul of modern Jewish humor is the Yiddish language. But before you can feel entirely at ease using Yiddish words, you should understand the *thought process* that created them. After all, long before there was Yiddish, there were Jews telling jokes in whatever language they could get their hands on. So, as the current saying goes, "Dress British, *think Yiddish.*"

"Vot is this craziness?" Or, to use the Yiddish word, "Vot is this *mishegas?*" Who cares about fishes? They smell. You can't even eat half of them. Yiddish, you may not know, is an incomplete language. It has no words for the several varieties of piranha or the viviparous eelpout. It is at a loss even to describe certain common flowers and trees. Provincial though it may be, Yiddish is not, however, snobbish. When the piranha becomes relevant or interesting enough it shall have a Yiddish name of its own. *Piranhakeit,* possibly. But enough for now of the language. It is merely a reflection of the thought pattern.

Thinking Yiddish is thinking in terms of the Big Putdown. Myron Cohen, the storyteller, made famous the joke about the tall Texan in the ten-gallon hat who had lost his way in a Jewish section of New York. He asked for directions.

"Pardner," he inquired of a passing pedestrian, "can yuh tell me where ah am?"

The man answered, "Boddy, you ain't in Marlboro Country."

The Big Putdown, sarcasm, call it what you will, Thinking Yiddish has become a common, everyday part of American semantics. It's a hard, white-knuckle grip on reality. It's plain but spicy sense in the face of bloated idealism and popular puffery. And it's fun.

Television has probably been the greatest vehicle for bringing Yiddish Thinking to the American public. The needling humor of Jewish comedians crackles in parlors and pubs across the country. Alan King puts down suburbia. Mort Sahl puts down the government. Jackie Leonard puts down everybody, and a man named Don Rickles very probably puts down Jackie Leonard. Woody Allen, who looks like a perennial bar mitzvah boy, puts down people who want to know if he's Jewish. "No," he says, "actually I'm an Orthodox Pervert." Even the Gentile comedians are now using Yiddish Thinking and Yiddish words, like kosher corned beef on white with mayonnaise.

Advertising has gone in big for Yiddish Thinking. For years, a man stood there on the TV and hit you over the head with reasons why you should buy his automobiles. He ranted and raved until you lay abject and earsore on your living room carpet. Finally, even Madison Avenue held its ears and wished for something more reasonable. So now what do you hear? "We're only number two," says a car rental service. "We try harder." Perhaps it was not a Jewish copywriter who thought up that idea, but place a "So" in front of each of those two sentences and you have a classic, self-deprecating Yiddish remark that humors the customer into doing business.

"Oh, the disadvantages" of smoking our extra-long one hundred millimeter cigarettes, laments another advertiser. Disadvantages? In the same way, a mother talks about the disadvantages of her daughter's thirty-eight-inch bust. In this country, anything that's big enough to get caught in elevator doors people are going to buy.

Everywhere the advertisements are enlisting our sympathies. A foreign auto maker apologizes for his ugly cars. A certain brand of tea tells us it isn't half bad. Another kind of cigarette admits it's not for everybody, and a snack food pleads for just one chance to get in our mouths. Oh, the groaning and the shrugging and the crying! Advertising, in case you haven't noticed it, is putting itself down, and the result, as people in the industry will confirm, is that Americans don't go to the toilet quite so much any more during the commercials. They are also buying a lot of snacks and automobiles.

The Yiddish Putdown has found its place in many professions. The law, accustomed to the solemn jargon of Latin, has, nevertheless, found frequent use for Yiddish Thinking. A lawyer friend tells of appearing in court against a youthful adversary whose plea was more notable for enthusiasm than habeas corpus. From his opening remarks, every experienced legal ear in the court surmised he had no case at all, yet listened politely to his long and tedious oration.

"Young man," said the judge, not unkindly. "What firm do you represent?" He gave the court a familiar and respected name.

The judge, a non-Jew, by the way, nodded. "Ah, yes," he said, "a most successful outfit. Now, what I would like you to do is return to your office and explain to the senior partners that the only way I could possibly judge this type of case would be if you were to submit a writ of *rachmonis* [the Yiddish word for pity]."

"I see," said the young lawyer, although obviously he did not, and then proceeded dutifully, no doubt, to carry out the court's instructions.

The Yiddish Putdown is based loosely on the following set of assumptions:

1) What is obvious is not worth discussing, and almost everything is obvious.

2) Aesthetics begin and end with the distinction between animal, vegetable and mineral.

3) Praise is intolerable except in the form of criticism.

4) Exaggeration is the secret of life.

Thus a Yiddish Thinking businessman replies over the phone to the complaints of one of his oldest and best customers: "Who is this? Mr. Wagner? Never heard of you!"

Or, as the Yiddish Thinking housewife tells the high-pressure appliance salesman: "If the vacuum cleaner is as beautiful as you say, then why isn't it hanging in the Museum of Modern Art?"

Or, as the Yiddish Thinking father applauds his son upon finishing medical school: "Congratulations. So now tell me what is the cure for cancer?"

Imagine the latitude and freedom of interpretation possible if we were to substitute the Yiddish Putdown for some of our traditional forms of praise and censure:

The letter of reference

Dear Brown;

I don't know why your company would be interested in Harold Beckman, a man who works for me fourteen years without a complaint then suddenly ups and looks for another position. This job-hopper probably told you he sold for me $10 million worth of goods. What kind of a strange, bashful duck tells you $10 million when he really sold $50 million? What's more, this Beckman is a sneak. You know he learned my business inside and out so well I could take six months in Jamaica without a worry in my head? What is he after? His personality you won't care for either. A drudge who works twelve hours a day and sweeps up when he leaves. If you still want to hire this man don't say I didn't warn you.

Yours truly,
Jones

A guide to the European traveler

The *first-class accommodations* in this small French city have nice warm, double-thick blankets and no smells in the corridors. You might even get a bun for breakfast. In *second-class hotels* you get a window, a clean sheet and a lot of German tourists in the next room hollering their heads off.

Third class is already a five-story walk-up and you'll spend all night staring at an animal on the ceiling.

Not the most objective system of evaluating things, perhaps, but a lot more stimulating than stars and letters.

How about the credibility gap? If people today really are overcommunicated yet underinformed, why not apply the Big Putdown to our most familiar outlets of public communication? The news, for instance:

Credibility Gap Headline	*Big Putdown Headline*
SENATE VETOES GUN BILL!	A NUT CAN STILL SHOOT YOU!
PRESIDENT'S SALARY DOUBLED!	AFTER TAXES, IT'LL BUY HIM A PEN AND PENCIL SET!
STUDENTS STORM CAMPUS!	NUDNIKS CARRYING BOOKS ARE STILL NUDNIKS!
ANOTHER LAKE POLLUTED!	TAKE A POLITICIAN SWIMMING!
TAXPAYERS TO PAY MORE!	THEY'LL HAVE TO SUCK OUR BLOOD OUT!

Speaking of headlines, newspapers recently reported the discovery of early American Indian trinkets bearing what seemed to be ancient Hebrew inscriptions. This led one anthropologist to suggest that long before Columbus and even Leif Ericson the New World had been found by daring adventurers of yet another culture. Jews had discovered America!

I overheard two Jewish men discussing the implications of this news.

"Hah!" exclaimed the first. "This confirms a theory I've held myself." He went on at some length in a not unfamiliar Jewish chauvinistic vein.

"But," the second man interrupted at last, "do you know what the inscriptions on the trinkets said?"

"Why, no," admitted the first.

"Prices slashed!"

The Power of Yiddish Thinking is the power to disarm an enemy or even a friend, for the very good purpose of warming him up, or bringing him down to earth.

An old and dear friend of mine recently passed through a deep soul-searching period of his life. He is a businessman, and basically a practical sort. But during this time he wrote a very long and touching letter full of poetry and philosophy, in which he compared his state to that of a man embarking on an ocean voyage, destination unknown. This analogy evidently becoming insufficient to express his thoughts, he then went on to speak of his life in terms of a fine clock that needed repairs. Although sympathetic to, and, as I said, touched by his remarks, I found it irresistible, because of the morose tone (for him) of the letter, to reply as a Yiddish Thinker.

Dear Bob,

You're going on a boat ride? What is this? You need a new clock? So buy one with a nice alarm, you can afford it. What kind of problems are these for a Jewish kid? Straighten up!

Marty.

As if I didn't understand. And Bob soon returned to his natural role of matter-of-fact, got-all-the-answers businessman.

Still another friend spent her childhood in a remote Australian city. She worshiped her uncle, a traveling man, who had seen the whole world and tasted many times over of its delights. She confessed to him that her great secret desire was to see Broadway. For one glimpse of that silver street she would gladly surrender her young life. At this, the uncle took her hand and led her to the main street of the town. He pointed up to a solitary electric sign advertising petrol in blue and red and orange.

"There," he said. "There it is."

"Whatever do you mean?" the child asked.

"There is Broadway," said the uncle, "only bigger."

A Yiddish Thinking man of very modest attainments died and left a will. To his wife he bequeathed stocks and bonds and foreign bank accounts (all imaginary, of course). The assembled family, appreciating the joke, applauded. To his daughter, who told me this story, he willed four blocks of valuable downtown real estate which were never his. A great cheer went up. To the sons went his "business," which, to the wild enthusiasm of the audience, encompassed a world-wide network of important enterprises. But, finally, to the family cat he left a sum of cash that was ten times the value of all the other gifts combined. The assembly sat stunned and, after a time, dispersed. But not before they heard the last words of the will: ". . . and if I could have afforded a dog, I'd give *him* everything I didn't give the cat!"

The Big Putdown. Effective even from the grave.

I personally play a little game of Putdown with friends which, I have no doubt, originated in some Yiddish thought. When I find that a formal or stuffy relationship is making me uncomfortable, I ask, with all apparent sincerity:

"Do you have any relatives in New York?" Almost invariably, the fellow proceeds not only to tally up every New York-abiding distant cousin, but to provide me with far more biographical information than my casual question called for. Or he may simply answer "Yes." In any case, my standard retort is "F____ 'em!"

Some of my best friendships began on this note of Yiddish Thinking.

2

YIDDISH DISRESPECT
or
Dear God, Cutie Pie

In our own time we have seen the fine old art of disrespect fall into disrepute. To the Yiddish Thinker, the reasons for this are both obvious and painful. In America today, disrespect has gotten into the hands of zealots and axe-grinders, both professional and amateur. It has become selective and sloganized and unfortunately, therefore, somewhat discredited. Policemen are "pigs," the complacent masses are a "silent majority," demonstrators are "effete snobs." People in general play a game of pitch and catch with epithets that have been packaged and approved like so many regulation baseballs.

Disrespect Yiddish-style is a horselaugh of a different color. It is absolute. It is devastating. It plays no favorites. It has, in short, a bad word (and usually many more than one) for everybody . . .

He's a millionaire? Marvelous. All his money should buy him a friend before he's in the ground.

The President is going to be on TV? Maybe next they'll put him in nightclubs.

Jackie Kennedy married Onassis? And I thought she was going to marry Mickey Mouse.

for every thing . . .
Yes, I see the badge, officer. Tell me, has it always been that size, or has it grown since you were born?

for every opinion . . .
Of course there is no freedom in the United States, son. And your father and I are members of the Gestapo.

Clearly, however, if no target is to be considered out of range, by the same rule no person shall be disqualified as a marksman. The mother who cuts down her son is fair game for the son:

Ma, you wouldn't recognize a fascist if he
goose-stepped all over your petunias.

If more people understood the rules of Yiddish disrespect, I think that bothersome term "the generation gap" might never have been conceived. Yiddish Thinking is available to young and old alike to be used upon each other in the interest of that best of all possible human relationships, a "healthy disrespect."

Consider this example of a young attorney discussing the settlement of a case with his elderly opponent, a wily and crotchety gut lawyer of the old school.

The young man patiently explained a recent point of law which seemed to give him an open-and-shut case. At this, the old-timer grumbled and snorted, making much of his vast experience with the law.

"Never heard of such a thing," he barked. "Seventy-five

years old. Been in this business fifty-two years . . ." Blah
blah blah.

"Tell you what," said the young lawyer. "When we go
before the judge, I'll bring the book of law and you bring your
birth certificate."

The proper Yiddish Thinker is simply not impressed by
age, argument and, perhaps least of all, by flattery.

Several years ago, according to a friend who worked there
at the time, an advertising agency serving Kaiser Industries
was hard put to think of an appropriate eightieth birthday
gift for the late Henry J. Kaiser, a remote and awesome
figure. After weeks of deep collective thought, the ad people
came up with the inspiration of commissioning the even
more elderly poet Carl Sandburg to compose an original
verse honoring the industrial titan on reaching his ninth
decade. This took some doing because the now deceased
poet was apparently not predisposed to penning hymns to per-
sonages—titans or otherwise—of less historical significance than
Abraham Lincoln. Finally, all parties concerned had to be
satisfied with a facsimile of the Sandburg style, rendered by
an artful copywriter, cursorily edited, and endorsed with his
best wishes by the prairie poet himself. Not quite what they
bargained for. But authentic enough.

When, at long last, the precious parchment was placed
into the tycoon's gnarled fingers, all in attendance held their
breath. Eyes that had foreseen the potentialities of aluminum
quickly scanned the hard angular prose. He looked up, or so
the story goes, and to his hushed and reverent audience
exclaimed, "Who's Carl Sandburg?"

Henry J. Kaiser was, of course, not a Jew. And, certainly,
few people have had as little need for self-inflation as this
dynastic figure. I doubt if it was ever ascertained whether
the old man really did or did not know the identity of the
poet Sandburg. Under the circumstances, who would dare to

ascertain it? And yet, sincere or not, the remark was a classic of Yiddish contempt.

The story told of Louis Armstrong, the great jazz trumpeter, in a command performance before the Swedish crown, is worth repeating here. Supposedly, the monarch requested a personal introduction to the famed musician. Some elaborate protocol ensued, during which His Majesty was formally presented. Now it was Mr. Armstrong's turn. In a flash of teeth the husky greeting came:

"Hi, king."

Nor is the Yiddish Thinker impressed by accomplishments. As a youth growing up in poverty, a now famous Hollywood producer was marked by friends and neighbors as one who would come to little in life. A letter to his mother telling of his first Hollywood assignment at $100 a week, a formidable salary in those early days, met only with cluckings from these same friends and neighbors. "*He* says a hundred dollars a week," they scoffed. "Knowing him, it's fifty."

A short time later the news arrived of a $300-a-week salary.

"*He* says three hundred dollars," they grumbled. "Knowing him, it's a hundred and fifty."

When, some time later, word arrived of his fantastic financial success as a producer—the incredible amount of $2,000 per week—still the Yiddish Thinkers scoffed.

"*He* says two thousand a week. Knowing this kid, it's four thousand!"

One of the best examples of Yiddish disrespect in recent years concerned a small black boy and a television clown. Disrespect for a clown? Why, certainly. Who does that guy think he is in those big flat shoes and that corny wig? The boy, a contestant, had just missed out on the big cash jackpot. And so, in the tense after-silence, he used a word unfamiliar to TV audiences.

"Shit," he said.

At this the MC got some kind of clown's apoplexy and began apologizing all over the airwaves for the boy's remark. Stone-faced, the youth stood by for just so much of this, and finally let him have it right between the polka dots.

"Cram it, clown," said the boy. And if he got spanked for it later, I'm certain there must have been a smile on his momma's face as she laid on the hairbrush.

Perhaps of all natural adversaries, husbands and wives who are Yiddish Thinkers provide us with examples of the "healthiest disrespect":

The Birthday Present

She: Ooh, I'm so excited. I hope it's as nice as your last gift. What was it, dear? A stuffed owl?

He: It was a feather boa.

She: Oh! Look! Lovely! Plastic slacks!

He: Vinyl. You'd know it if you'd been following the fashions for the past five or ten years.

She: Marvelous. And in my mother's size.

He: That's true. Houdini was a twerp at getting out of things compared to the way your mother gets into them.

She: Why, you must have spent as much as ten minutes shopping for this.

He: It's not the thought, but the price behind it.

She: Well, it's just what I would've always wanted if I were twelve years old.

He: So why complain? You'll be able to wear it in just a couple of years!

The Bank Statement

He: Excuse me, dear, but how could you subtract eighty-nine dollars from ninety-five and get a balance of eleven dollars and thirty-three cents?

She: I lied to you when we were married, honey. I wasn't a mathematician.

He: Ah, that explains this deposit of five hundred and inkblot dollars.

She: Have me arrested, darling, my pen leaks.

He: No, I forgive you if you'll just explain this two-hundred-and-fifty-dollar check to the milkman.

She: Certainly, sweetheart. Thirty dollars milk. Twenty dollars eggs. And two hundred gigolo money!

He: Well, you'll be happy to know that thanks to you we have only a hundred-dollar overdraft this month.

She: An overdraft, dear? Isn't that something you catch if you don't wear underwear?

Spring Cleaning

He: I suppose you want me to wash the windows.

She: No, I want you to throw dirt on them.

He: I'd clean the basement but I can't get in.

She: Burn it.

He: You've got a thousand dead corsages up here in the attic. What should I do with them?

She: Smell 'em.

He: Well, I've done so much work already I think it's time for a break.

She: Certainly, dear. Will it be an arm or a leg?

Poets, kings, clowns, husbands, wives, nobody in the world is immune to Yiddish irreverence. Yiddish Thinking allows you to approach even the Almighty in fresh, provocative terms:

Dear God, cutie pie, this is a clever trick you're playing on me, but personally I like you better as a religious figure than a practical joker.

God, I know you're a busy person, but you've paid about as much attention to me lately as my second cousins—those *kockers*—in Hoboken.

God in heaven. You parted the Red Sea. You made water from a stone. Fire from a bush even. You couldn't get my brother Herschel to fork up the fifty bucks he owes me?

Or, as Tevyeh the poor dairyman inveigled so much more poetically in *Fiddler on the Roof*:

> Lord who made the lion and the lamb,
> would it spoil some vast eternal plan
> if I was a wealthy man?

"Your merchandise is worth to me a little bit of crap and two whistles."—Sam Mevorah

3

THE FLAT STATEMENT
or
No Such Item. Never Was. Never Will Be

The next step in acquiring the Power of Yiddish Thinking is to familiarize yourself with what we will call "The Flat Statement." In most systems of logic, generalities are frowned upon. If you were to say, for example, "Children should be seen and not heard," no doubt you would be taken to task by intelligent parents who see the need for children to express themselves on frequent occasions. The Yiddish Flat Statement goes beyond such generalities. It is outrageous, wildly exaggerated, perverse and frequently has no basis whatever in fact. About children, to follow our previous example, such a Flat Statement might be: "Children are bums." This kind of remark, uttered with wholehearted conviction, is based on the idea unique to Yiddish Thinking known as *chutzpah*,* the nerve to say what will set things straight in the face of overwhelming sentiment to the contrary.

* See Chapter 4.

Ulysses is a lousy story.
Nuns sweat a lot.
Swimming is boring.
Fat people look young.
Career women are frigid.
The best medicine is chicken soup.

Obviously, nobody can argue with statements like these. How can you call chicken soup medicine? For what sickness is chicken soup good medicine? Why chicken soup . . . why not onion soup? Such questioning is useless in the face of a Flat Statement. It is cleverly calculated to undermine all logic. For instance, if anyone dared to question the remark, say, about nuns, your answer would simply be another Flat Statement:

Poor things, with all those clothes they wear and no air conditioning . . .

The effect of this kind of Yiddish Thinking is absolutely to cut off all unnecessary conversation and discourage subjects which are of little interest to you.

Let us say your arch competitor at the office just got a fabulous new assignment in Rio de Janeiro. Your own job demands that you remain in Akron, Ohio, for the next fifteen years. He is virtually dancing about the premises, unable to disguise his good fortune. The conversation that ensues is not likely to hold many thrills for you. So you begin with a Flat Statement:

"Don't worry. I read where you've got a fifty-fifty chance of not getting amoebic dysentery."

To this he logically rebuts, "You're mistaken, friend, that's Mexico, not Brazil."

But he is as yet not aware that he is up against a Yiddish Thinker.

"A Spanish germ doesn't know from national borders."

He thinks he's got you. "Oh, come now. And anyway, Rio isn't Spanish-speaking."

"Worse," you put in. "In their language who knows what they call it. It's probably even deadlier."

Still he does not surrender. "Well," he admits, "once you catch one of these bugs and get over it, they say you don't have to worry any more."

And now you are ready with a Flat Statement bearing the weight and finality of a coffin lid. "That's true," you sigh, "and I suppose it's a nice comfort when you're living in a country where they consider twenty-five a ripe old age."

Once again, popular comedians supply us with prize examples of Yiddish Thinking in action.

The wild, free associations of humorists like Mel Brooks and Milt Kamin wring laughs out of subjects that seem humor-proof. After a trip through the expansive western United States, city boy Kamin once reported that there is no such place as Wyoming. Brooks, as nimble a comic mind as there is today, fires Flat Statements like a Jewish machine gun. The real secret of a long life, he has said, is to stay out of small foreign cars. Or you might have heard him State Flatly that the greatest technological achievement in all of history is plastic food wrap!

Don't think for a moment that the Yiddish Flat Statement is the exclusive tool of professional comedians and joke writers. It is the common, everyday psychology of people—mothers, teachers, merchants—who must often sacrifice pure truth for expediency. For instance, at the annual family dinner, your five-year-old daughter asks her grandmother, "What are birth control pills?" As a non-Yiddish Thinking mother you have two alternatives. One, take the whole family through a dreary clinical explanation on the spot. Two, think of something clever like this: "Birth control pills, dear, are what ladies take to keep from getting . . . nervous." In this situation, the Yiddish Thinking mother simply inverts the logic of the child's innocent question, retorting sharply, "I'll tell you what they are. They're poison. You swallow one of them and you're dead."

Sex, a subject of little interest generally to the Yiddish Thinker,* has been responsible for many an interesting Flat Statement. As a teenager, a friend of mine suffered terribly from adolescent acne. His young face was a mask of those awful sores and swellings that often scar the senses as well as the skin. Confused already by a family in which no word about sex was ever uttered, the poor kid was becoming wretched with anxieties. One day, without warning, his father turned to him, fixed him in the eye, held the face in his two hands and said, "Ven you have a voman, that all goes." And he did, and it did. Instant sex education!

Let's say you are a retail merchant. A customer requests an item you don't carry, but for which you can offer him an equally good substitute. Business is business, after all, and instead of referring the customer to your nearest competitor, it is quite acceptable, according to Yiddish Thinking, to shake your head knowingly and say, "There is no such item. Somebody gave you a bum goose." If this explanation should prove unconvincing, the Yiddish Thinker merely provides arguments of flatter and flatter contour. He may assume a technological expertise:

If it was possible to make such a marvelous article like you are describing, we would both know, like Benjamin Franklin, what is the name of the inventor.

* See Chapter 8.

And to all this, he might add the garnish of clairvoyance:
That we'll both get heart transplants and live to be a
hundred and fifty today I don't question it. Even then I
wouldn't be able to help you with this so-called item.

At this point in the battle of wills, I have been present
myself when the customer actually produced an advertisement
for the product in question and heard in reply:
Well, there's just no call for an item like this!

Perhaps the most fertile breeding ground for Flat Statements
is the retail atmosphere, where, after all, the factual is less
important than the negotiable.

A friend's family operated for many years a successful
drygoods establishment in a small Wisconsin town populated
by rural folk with little money to spend. The competition
down the street was barely able to sell enough spools of
thread and hanks of cheap cloth to keep their doors open.
The merchandise in both places was of virtually the same
quality and neither offered price advantages over the other.
And yet his family's business flourished.

"Pssst. Mrs. Jones, I got here something special for you."

"Ain't got but two dollars to spend."

"It's plenty."

"It won't buy silk."

"Who says? Here is silk, only two dollars and twenty-five."

"It's real silk?"

"*Rare*, missus. Dot's even better than real. It's what they
call the real, rare *misha mishina* silk."

"Mish . . . ?"

"I promise you, this they don't have down the street."

"Then where does it come from?"

"Dot's right. From Arabs could be it comes. From special

chinamen, maybe? They're living in pagodals making one
piece in a year."
"Y'mean to tell me it's imported?"
"I'm meaning to tell you only a *Chalyicher* could make a
piece cloth like this."
"Well, it's right purty, sure enough."
"In a dress from this material, Mrs. Jones, please listen
to me, you'll stand out around here like Lady Godiva
herself."

And sure enough, in that humble community, for years the
best dressed woman turned up in *misha mishina* silk, fashioned
—it seemed possible at least—by remote craftsmen known as
Chalyichers. Or in equally fine raiments of *betgevante* crepe
fringed with authentic *tsotskehs.* Indeed, such purchases became a sign of high taste and a source of social satisfaction in
a place where it was otherwise impossible to achieve these
necessary distinctions.

Another friend, a pharmacist, tells of being "shopped."
The customer, clutching a vial of patent medicine, asks:
"And what do you get for this?"
"The price is on the label," says the pharmacist.
"But it says two ninety-five. This is a fair price?"
"God himself wouldn't sell it for less."
"God maybe not, but Levin, down the street, is asking
only two sixty-five."
"In that case," the druggist replies, "I recommend you
buy it from Levin and pray for his starving family."
"But I can't get it there," the shopper shrugs, "he's all
out of it."
"Aha!" says my friend. "When I'm out of this item it's only
a dollar ninety-eight!"

If anyone cares to dissect them, he will discover a kind of outrageous honesty in remarks such as these. Not to mention a healthy personal anarchy, which, for better or worse, is the only kind left in the world.

Are you in need of a little personal anarchy? Are there some "profound" issues you hate to discuss? Are you bothered by bores, cranks and pseudo-intellectuals? Think of what you might say in the way of a Flat Statement. Here are a few suggestions to get you started:

> Toilet training is overrated.
> Europe is a clip joint.
> Smoking is good for you.
> Interior decorating is un-American.

We live in a world of sign language. We are told to Stop, Walk, Don't Walk, Fasten Seat Belts and so on. But do we really pay attention to such cold abbreviations? The scolding tone of the Yiddish Flat Statement could upgrade the public conscience, and along with it, public safety.

> WALK NOW IF YOU WANT A TRUCK
> TIRE ACROSS YOUR BACK.

> STOP, YOU SHOULDN'T HIT A LITTLE KIDDIE
> AND SPEND THE REST OF YOUR LIFE IN GRIEF!

> SMOKERS: IF YOU WANT TO POISON YOUR BODIES,
> COMMIT SUICIDE AT HOME, NOT IN A THEATER!

> RAILROAD CROSSING. YOU'LL LOOK 20 MILES
> IN EACH DIRECTION, A TRAIN IS FASTER THAN YOU THINK!

> MORE THAN 60 MPH, A TIRE BLOWS OUT
> AND YOU'RE GEHOCKTEH FLAISH!

SHUT UP. THE PEOPLE IN THIS HOSPITAL
HAVE ENOUGH TROUBLES THEY DON'T NEED
A LOT OF NOISE!

A Flat Statement, you see, not only presumes guilt, it presumes stupidity, negligence and foolishness. And who would
argue that a little more presumption of this type could save
us all a lot of grief?

"Tell the doctor he can see me now."—Milt Stern

4

CHUTZPAH
or
Of Big Shots, Long Shots and Short Cuts

"Don, you vouldn't believe it," said the ten-year-old boy. "Nah. You vouldn't pos'ble believe it."

"What wouldn't I believe?" asked my friend, who was a counselor of underprivileged boys, many of whom were recent immigrants to this country.

"Don," said the youth in dead earnest, "vould you believe dot I vasn't born in Chicageh?"

With such an attitude going for him, I believe that's one underprivileged kid who by now is a very well-privileged adult.

Chutzpah. What is it really? In the previous chapter we referred to it as something spoken, a nervy statement. But chutzpah is an idea bigger than words or thoughts or deeds alone. It is an approach to life which might be the single most important element of Yiddish Thinking except that it is a talent, as well, and few can claim it. Pure chutzpah is not a conscious attitude. It can be learned the way some athletes, not blessed with natural skills, accomplish through practice a degree of professional expertise. But, as in sports, the best marks go to the naturals, the form players of chutzpah.

The true creature of chutzpah has no regard for the probabilities of life. He is a chronic bettor of long shots. He is insensitive to risks. But his special grace is that he is almost never, despite his reckless behavior, made to appear a fool. In the end, there is method to his madness.

A working girl of my acquaintance bears an amazing resemblance to the popular TV entertainer and recording star Eydie Gormé. This coincidence and a little chutzpah have brought her a bonanza of soup mix and fresh vegetables.

"That's right," she informed the corner grocer one day, "I am Eydie Gormé." He had been pressing her for days to confess it.

"I knew it!" he shouted. "Eydie Gormé!" And immediately heads turned and a buzz began buzzing throughout the store.

"Eydie Gormé shops in *my* store," whispered the grocer, "Eydie Gormé gets a special treatment, hah?" He winked. The grocer was true to his word. For a year, the young secretary's masquerade brought her a cornucopia of free or discounted merchandise, until one day she observed, "It's amazing, isn't it, what people will do for a celebrity."

The grocer shrugged.

"Do you listen to . . . er . . . my records a lot?" she asked.

"Never," he said. "I don't care for that kind singing. The Lennon Sisters I like better."

Now the girl was really perplexed.

"Well, if you don't care for Eydie . . . I mean for my singing, why all this special treatment?"

"Trill seekers, vot else?" said the storekeeper. "A celebrity shops in my store, everybody shops in my store. Good for business. If you're Eydie Gormé or the Smothers Brothers, I personally couldn't care less."

The young woman decided to confess. "Listen, I must tell you I'm not really Eydie Gormé."

"Sure, I know it," said the grocer.

"You've known it all along?" The girl was flabbergasted.

"Sveetheart," the man sighed, "you're not Eydie Gormé and I'm not John Vayne either. But if the *shmegehgehs* who shop in this neighborhood vant to think so, who are ve to spoil their enjoyment?"

Chutzpah, like love, is a many-splendored thing.

To the Yiddish Thinker the world is an outrageous place, and to find comfort in it requires outrageous behavior. Not anti-social, not criminal certainly, but behavior that frequently departs from "polite" standards. In a word, chutzpah.

Unfortunately, chutzpah is one element of Yiddish Thinking that cannot be distilled into a set of simple rules. Nor can you, as a new YT, just go out and begin practicing chutzpah on the street. All I can do in this case is to provide classic examples to be scrutinized, as one stands before great works of art for hours in order to appreciate fully their beauty. Only with this appreciation will you be able to apply it, tentatively, to contemporary life.

Chutzpah for poor people

During the Depression, a favorite aunt of mine had only chutzpah to rely on as a means of augmenting her family's paltry income. Her husband, a police officer, could find extra work a couple of afternoons a week while she took the wheel of his patrol car, threw the baby in the back seat, and calmly cruised his beat! Had she been called upon to perform some police action in her husband's place, knowing her as I do, I'm certain she'd have carried that off with equal aplomb.

This same woman, finding herself in severe need of dental work but unable to pay, is said to have visited the dentist for a checkup one day and, while he had stepped from the office for a moment, "borrowed" some of his tools and materials. Later, the story goes, she performed the needed dental work on herself at home, returning the equipment. Whatever you may think, I have always believed this story. But let us go on.

Chutzpah for the lonely

Are you stuck in Paducah, Kentucky, caring for an invalid granny? Is your love life limited to an exchange of wistful glances with the local druggist? Are you obliged to live alone in a lighthouse until you are thirty-five in order to collect an inheritance? The world does crazy things to make us lonely but, again, when there seems to be no way out, there is always chutzpah.

No one ever had more of it than those immigrant Jewish men who, barely familiar with the language, roamed throughout small-town America in the early part of the century, peddling their wares from door to door. And who has ever been as lonely as they must have been plodding strange roads between even stranger places with Gentile names like Jefferson City or Dubuque? I know the story of one such man who, after years of such wandering, found himself at last weary and near frozen to death, alone in the streets of some God-forsaken city in remote North Dakota. The end of the line, for him. He found the local barber shop, inquiring there if any Jewish families resided in the community. Yes, he was told, there were two.

"Any dotters?" he asked succinctly.

Yes, again. Both families had a daughter, he was informed.

"These are married?" he asked.

Neither, indeed, was married, as it happened, and so,

properly evaluating the odds, he set out to marry the first girl who would have him. And, sure enough, after a good hot meal and a minimum of amenities, it developed that the first girl would. HE TURNED HER DOWN FLAT! Was he so sure the second woman was prettier? Or a better cook? Or whatever? And even if she were, how could he know she would accept him? Well, she did. And that, my friends, is chutzpah!

Chutzpah for the old

Perhaps you've already noticed how Yiddish Thinking has a special bias for the old. Where most cultures chuckle apologetically and clear their throats with embarrassment in the presence of their old folks, contrariwise, Yiddish Thinking draws much of its inspiration from this very source. And this is quite natural, for who survives from day to day like the old? And what age is so sensitive to the brutish winds of change as old age? Indeed, the old might be the most defenseless minority group of all . . . were it not for the tools of Yiddish Thinking.

The Yiddish Thinker of advanced years may turn the very prejudices he faces to his own advantage. A friend tells this story of his maiden great-aunt during the years of Prohibition. Language-limited and too old to work, the dear old lady had only the economic support of her distant family to keep her spirit alive in the dwindling days of her life. Food, clothing and the custom of preparing ritual wine each year at Passover, were her only comforts. The sweet wine she brewed in her cellar, exempt as this religious practice was from the strictures of the era. Somehow it entered the thoughts of this venerable person that her skills as a vintner might attract the interest of certain of her neighbors in the transient district in which she lived. And, sure enough, before long she was celebrating Passover throughout the year in the company of all manner of fascinating clientele. Dry-tongued sailors fresh out of boot camp. Out-of-work bartenders. Day laborers, street women, Chinese laundrymen, the postman and the local parish priest all shared the ritual cup with old Aunt Rochel. And although sociability was her major aim, she would look the other way at carry-out requests while extending her palm, understandably, for some small cash recognition of her service to the community.

"Bootlegger! By God, the old crank is a bootlegger!" As you might have guessed, the authorities were chagrined by the discovery of Aunt Rochel's offbeat hospitality. But not nearly so chagrined as when she offered her defense.

"A religious occasional. Postively, dot's all!"

Come now, old woman, a religious observance with the U.S. fleet? A Catholic priest? A Chinaman?

"You mean . . ." And with the badge-disintegrating concentration of some crude laser beam, the old woman rejoined, "You mean they're not JEWISH?" You may say they freed her because she was old, eccentric, addlebrained or uncomprehending. I say chutzpah.

Another friend's aged grandfather, a butcher, owned a shop in a tough section of town. Fearing robberies, he kept only a small amount of cash in the register, sequestering the largest part of his money in the meat locker among the carcasses. Sure enough, one day, alone in the shop, he was held up.

"Open the register, or I'll blow your head off," demanded the gunman.

"Whatever you want, it's yours," said the old man, turning over the meager contents of the cash drawer. "Getting mine head blown off I don't need."

But the robber wasn't fooled. "Come on, grandpa," he snarled, "show me where you keep the real dough or I'll blast you full of holes."

"Have a rump roast, a dozen nice lean lamb chops, anything, dot's all what I got I promise you. Just no holes, please."

"Okay," said the desperado, "you just climb into that locker while I have a look around."

"This I couldn't do," said the old-timer. "Absolutely, positively not."

There was no time to argue, and the robber hurried off. But not before he heard the old man say, "I should go into a freezer and catch a cold?"

But before you dismiss chutzpah as a talent beyond your chromosomes, remember I said it could also be developed, and there are plenty of real-life success stories to substantiate this.

A very famous Hollywood impresario grew up in poverty. As a youth he worked for small wages and tips as a busboy in a large metropolitan hospital. They were hard times, and the busboy business was one of the hardest hit. In fact, tips could be expected only from a certain grouping of luxury rooms set aside for well-to-do patients. In one of these rooms a surly man—the scion of a rich and powerful family—lay sick near death with cirrhosis of the liver. Several busboys had already been seen flying from the room on the seat of their pants, when he decided to try his luck with the ill-tempered patient.

"They won't get me any booze!" the man barked.

"But that would kill you, sir," the youth protested weakly.

"With or without it I'm going to kick the bucket," snarled the man. "God, let a drunk die drunk."

The boy paused a moment and then said, "What you need, sir, is a bottle of booze."

Shortly after the man died, the boy received his "tip." A letter came from the family, glowing with endearments and gratitude for the young man who brought some comfort (they knew not what kind) to the last days of their dear departed's existence, and stuffed with a check for $1,000. Furthermore, said the letter, if the darling boy ever in his life needed assistance, financial or otherwise, he had only to turn to the grateful . . . etcetera, etcetera.

And, creature of chutzpah that he was, all of his life he did turn to the family, as I said, becoming tremendously successful as a theatrical producer. Is the story true? I don't know, but I heard it from one of the busboys who was sent flying on the seat of his pants.

The head of one of the world's largest clothing manufacturers discovered the value of chutzpah early in his career. As a Gentile working in a very Jewish industry, he recognized certain obstacles to hasty promotion in his chosen field. Much of the important shoptalk was exchanged in Yiddish—as it still is in the business today. A lesser man in his position would have attempted a study of the language. But mysterious opportunities were flying by daily. Cryptic intelligences escaped his understanding, all of which he knew had imminent bearing on his success or failure in a fast-moving business.

No, it was a time for long-shots, short-cuts or, better still—if he had known the word then—chutzpah. And so this wandering Protestant reached back and tapped some hoary Anglo-Saxon wisdom which told him about the newspaper. Of course! The Yiddish newspaper!

He carried it every day thereafter, folded conspicuously in his hip pocket. And though he spoke nary a word of Yiddish no competitor would dare assume he did not understand!

"Jerusalem? I was born there. Jaffa? I was born there, too!"—T. Neustadt

5

THE MEGILLA
or
The Truth, Not Plain and Simple

If you seek the naked truth, you are wasting your time with Yiddish Thinking. Nudity of any kind offends the proper Yiddish Thinker. On the contrary, Yiddish Truth typically appears in full habit, elaborately laced, girdled, scarved and overcoated. For the truth, like small Jewish boys, is too delicate to be sent out into the cold world without its earmuffs.

You want to know why I was late again for work today? Well, as you can guess, my bus was not hijacked to Cuba this morning. The mailman did not give me a stock tip which caused me to convert all my investments to cash before 9 A.M. I was not seized and searched at the newsstand as a suspected dope peddler. I did, if you're interested, for the third morning in a row, *shlep* myself from bed, take double the dose prescribed of my anti-pneumonia medication, wait forty-five minutes for the bus in snow up to

my *pipik*, and black out in the elevator so that I might—
even though twenty minutes late—complete some reports
which not one of my co-workers, all in the best of health,
could possibly accomplish as well for the continued success
and profitability of our beloved, *verkockteh* company.

Is the truth less truthful if also interesting, complex and
open to infinite interpretation? The Yiddish Thinker considers
truth hardly worth telling if unaccompanied by all related
contributory and potential evidence. "The truth rests with
God alone," says an old Jewish adage, "and a little with me."

This unique reserve clause puts the Yiddish Thinker literally
in a class by himself. He is not the simple bore who is
asked the time and explains the workings of a watch. He has
at his command a most useful conversational ploy known as
the *megilla*, literally the great scroll containing thousands
of years of Jewish law; practically an engaging alternative
to unnecessary candor.

Frequently, a megilla begins with a generous recounting of
the un-truth, as with our grumpy friend who was late for
work. This tends immediately both to disparage the ques-
tioner and the need for his question. At the same time, by
such ridiculous contrast, it promotes the conviction of one's
eventual answer when one finally gets to it.

For another instance, think of how you might answer a
neighbor who wants to know if it was your dog (and it was)
who entered his house and ate his furniture. A fine time to
apply the negative megilla.

"The dog who ate four hundred dollars worth of your
upholstery died two days ago, if it was a dog. After all, a dog
isn't a termite. On mahogany he croaks. A vet doesn't recommend goose down. My own dog he wouldn't even touch a
filet mignon he's got a digestion like the King of France.

"As for going into somebody else's house, like most animals my dog doesn't have fingers for turning knobs and he's not a mouse that he can crawl up through the drainpipe. If the door is always left wide open so burglars and whoknowswhat can walk right into a house, a dog doesn't have a brain like you and me to know he's not invited. So maybe he did chew a little bit on the varnish, it looked to him like a chicken leg. This style of chair I don't think is a four-hundred-dollar item in the first place, maybe something like ninety-nine ninety-five . . . and when you think a two-hundred-dollar dog didn't get furniture poisoning with a fifty-dollar funeral in addition you know you came out ahead with just a simple lesson to keep the doors closed in your house."

One lady of my acquaintance, a fine Yiddish Thinker, always opens a telephone conversation with the negative megilla.

Hello. I don't suppose Mrs. Frankel is at home? She is? Then she's probably not free to talk? She can? Hello, this couldn't be Mrs. Frankel? Oh. Well, since you haven't phoned me in over six months I guess you wouldn't be interested in hearing some news about a mutual friend? You would? Etcetera, etcetera.

On the other hand, the megilla can be flamboyantly positive. One time my own phone rang at 4 A.M. It was a Yiddish Thinking friend:

Don't bother taking off your pajamas. Throw on a coat and get in your car. Drive a hundred miles an hour to Fisher's Furniture. You're looking for a hide-a-bed? By Fisher's, a sale on hide-a-beds is starting at 8 A.M., not in a thousand years would you have such an opportunity. A limited supply, and by one minute after eight the whole city will be there. You'll park four blocks from the store and run

you shouldn't waste time looking for parking space closer
in. Don't talk. Fly. Later you'll kiss me. Good-bye."

Incredible as it seems, I followed this advice to the letter.
The megilla had its effect, although for what purpose I don't
know. I found at Fisher's one sleepy-eyed salesclerk, vast
showrooms filled to the ceilings with discounted hide-a-beds
and, of course, not even one breathless, bargain-crazed pajama
wearer like myself. And yet, it seems to me, any sales or
advertising man reading this can take a lesson in timing,
enthusiasm and conviction from a good old-fashioned Yiddish
megilla.

Megillas may take many different forms and styles. They
may be dietetic. When I was a child, my mother once
convinced me that vegetable soup was indispensable if I was
to live to the age of twelve.

"Eat," she insisted. "The orange things are carrots. We must
eat them to have good eyesight. Blindness I wouldn't wish on
anyone, let alone my own son. The green slippery things are
celery. Loaded with iron. Without iron you'll be so weak
you couldn't even wiggle one toe I promise you. What white
stuff? That's potatoes. Starch. Every person should have
some fat on his bones he shouldn't freeze in winter. If a boy
doesn't eat vegetable soup he might as well commit suicide,
and then his mother—what does she have to live for?—kills herself too. A double funeral, the relatives crying, wailing, and
the rabbi says 'all because the boy didn't like the looks of
vegetable soup.'"

A megilla may be diplomatic, as when someone asks who you
voted for in the last presidential election:

"I'll tell you. Hubert Humphrey reminded me exactly of my
uncle Herschel, a man who would give you the shirt off his
back, except his shirt was a twenty-year-old *shmateh* you
wouldn't even wear it out to the garage. A nice fella with a

wonderful smile it never earned him a nickel. Now, you take this Nixon, here is a man with nervous eyes like any minute someone is going to sneak up and goose him, he talks like a registered nurse, 'Now, Now, Mr. Country, we've got some nice pills for your condition, please turn over and we'll take the temperature.' Who knew what he would stick in there?

"The other one what they call Wallace was hollering so much at everybody it's a dead image of my neighbor Rose, with a body that's ninety per cent mouth. Four years of this and we'll have a deaf country on top of all the other problems. Not that I'm such a family type individual, but when it comes to a choice for President between a male nurse with funny eyes and a mouth with legs, I'll take the shirt from Uncle Herschel and I'll wear it in the Easter Parade."

The megilla has no rival in other cultures or languages as an argumentative device. For instance, the French, well-known for their volubility and particularly for their flamboyant manual oratory, have no tool to match the relentless web-spinning logic of the megilla. Imagine a confrontation—assuming no language barrier—between the familiar figure of the intimidating Parisian hotel clerk and the solid Yiddish Thinker.

Waving his arms, the Frenchman speaks in excited ejaculations. He is trying to tell our YT that his bill is twice the amount of the agreed-upon rate and theatens to call the gendarmes.

"Frenchie," the Yiddish Thinker begins, quietly enough, "you know what is the groin? The groin is the second most important place a person has in his body. It's where you make . . . and if you can't make you'll fill up inside and die from Uremia. It's also where you have fun with what is called 'sex,' which is supposed to be your big specialty here, although I'm not convinced myself, I see your men are traipsing around the boulevards with canes singing, 'Thank heaven for little girls.' Well, I'm sure you know that the first most important part of the body is the head, because you people are always chopping it off on a guillotine when somebody makes a crime and you can have mine too if you want it. But only if you have here a French law where they can decapitate me in the other section what I said, then will you get the kind of money you are talking about, *boobeleh*."

Like a home-cooked Jewish meal, the megilla offers you two courses more than you can eat while forcing you to apologize for a lack of appetite.

Enormous megillas, of cosmic scope and meaning, have been unloosed over the simplest and most casual of remarks. One extremely cold winter day recently a bachelor friend discovered that the top button of his brown overcoat was missing. At a nearby tailor shop he asked the proprietor to match a button and sew it on.

"Vun brown button coming up," he said cheerfully, beginning his search in a tower of old shoe boxes. "Life insurance is a button. Sure! On a day like this a vind goes down on the open chest and soon a cough comes. But some cough! A killer cough! From the germs, too. Vit the pellution . . . who is doing something about it?"

Exhausting the shoe box tower, he turned to a pile of battered tea tins. "Nobody cares today. You'll get your killer cough and in the hospital there's so many people from the explosion you'll be lucky if they take from you a temperature let alone give a bed. They got patients now sleeping six, eight together, doesn't matter vut disease they got.

"Nah. Vut do they care? They got no time to teach the doctors anymore." He climbed a wall to search through some dusty cigar boxes. "An Indian from India fourteen years old is a doctor. They give him a needle and a pill and they say, 'Go, there's a man with a killer cough.'

"Feh! They got so many people in the world now, you

could give half of them your disease and the other half vouldn't know they're missing.

"Meanwhile, no vonder people are so nervous today." He was in the back room now, fumbling among ancient jelly glasses and coffee cups. "Dumping nerve gas in the vater! Who are they kidding? A gas doesn't stay in the vater. It goes anyvhere it vants, in your nose or under your fingernails. And imagine them bringing back that dirt—*shmutz*—from the moon! You think moondirt is going to stay under that microscope? It's probably got legs, feelers . . . it valks on you there's no cure for it."

At long last, the tailor reappeared from the shadows in back of the store, clutching the coat. "Here. Like I say, a button is life insurance today."

"But," my friend hesitated, finding his voice, "you've sewn on a black button!"

"Sonny." From somewhere deep down in his soul the old man invoked a sigh of tolerance. "Ven every breath you are taking has a pellution vit a nerve gas on top of a moon germ mixed vit a nookler radioactivity, you think it matters the color from a button?"

There is yet another tactic available to the Yiddish Thinker in his indirect approach to the truth. When the Flat Statement will not suffice and the megilla does not apply, one may participate in a kind of conversational Ping-Pong in which questions are met only with counter questions:

"Does your husband remember your anniversary?"
"Does my husband remember to zip his pants in the morning?"
"What did he give you last year?"
"What does a stone give to a bird?"
"Didn't you ask for a mink coat?"
"Is God a furrier?"

"Well, doesn't he ever bring you gifts?"
"Does Cary Grant call me for weekends on the Riviera?"
Etcetera, etcetera.

Note that a complete dialogue is possible in which one arrives at conclusions which allow no possibility of being quoted. Think of the political ramifications.

"Mr. President, do you think the income surtax will be repealed before long?"
"Does a chicken live a hundred years?"
"What will you do if there's another long hot summer?"
"What would you do if your wife got piles on your honeymoon?"
"Do you see an end to inflation?"
"Can you see a flea on a dog?"
"Will you stop the Selective Service system?"
"Will your grandmother fire a submachine gun?"

Incredibly, all the questions have been resolved, but there is *no record* of the answers. No cogent record, at least. If the Yiddish question-and-question period ever became the rule for presidential press conferences it would tax the skills of the most lucid journalists.

Queried on the possible discontinuation of Selective Service, the President today speculated on the willingness of America's senior citizens to operate heavy military equipment.

Which make no sense at all.
Obviously, there is no quoting or even paraphrasing the Yiddish question/answer. You just have to *be* there. In Yiddish Thinking anything you say may not be held against you.

6

YIDDISH OPTIMISM
or
A Cure for Yale and Gallbladder

By now you may be convinced that Yiddish Thinking is nothing more than a chronic pessimism, a kind of mental in-
digestion. Its value seems to be entirely deflationary, rather
like having a porcupine in your mouth. Actually, the same
techniques so well fashioned for bubble bursting are uniquely
suited for bubble mending. The Utopian has not yet been
born who can match the well-grounded Yiddish Thinker rosy
notion for rosy notion. How can this be? It does seem con-
tradictory, and so a thorough explanation is in order.

Let us briefly review the mental requirements of the Yiddish
Thinker: 1) he must be unimpressible; 2) he ignores fine
distinctions; 3) he ignores large distinctions; 4) he rejects the
obvious; 5) he can predict the future.

There's an old story—and that's not what you're here for—
but one so apt that I can't resist repeating it in this context.
Two Jewish ladies meet on the street and one says: "Did you
hear about Hyman Feldstein?"

THE POWER OF YIDDISH THINKING

The second lady thinks and says, "You don't mean the Hyman Feldstein with the twisted leg?"

"The same," says the first lady.

"He's the one with the bad eye and the cough, isn't he?"

"That's him," repeats the first lady.

"Sure, I know him. He always had a funny skin and some bone condition, too," recalled the second lady. "So what about him?"

"He died," says the first lady.

"Oy!" groans the second lady, "such a healthy man."

Now, for a more contemporary example, let's say your son is in jail, apparently having been picked up for curfew violation. As a practicing Yiddish Optimist, you tell the arresting officer:

"The boy walks in his sleep. A curfew can't stop this."

"He was driving."

"So? He's a clever boy."

"He was driving a stolen car."

"Boys will be boys."

"He was wearing a dress."

"Ah, but not a *stolen* dress."

"And he was under the influence of both alchohol and marijuana."

"At least something influences him."

"He'll get a stiff sentence for this."

"Whew! Then he's innocent!"

"Innocent?"

"He didn't pull the trigger."

"But there was no shooting."

"Of course— So how long can you keep an innocent kid in jail?"

Yiddish optimism frequently has a medical flavor. Health, like anything else basic to survival, is a major preoccupation of the Yiddish Thinker. And he is a born doctor. Consider this conversation overheard between two patients in a hospital room.

Bed one: How much longer you have to stay here?

Bed two: Six weeks, the doctor said.

Bed one: What he says! Three, the most.

Bed two: The scar isn't healing.

Bed one: That's a scar? It's a mosquito bite!

Bed two: It was a gallbladder, after all.

Bed one: A gallbladder is a nothing. You don't even need it.

Bed two: Well, it hurts plenty I can tell you.

Bed one: They've got pills here better than LSD. You want to go to the moon? Give the nurse a winky, she'll take care of you.

Bed two: The pills don't seem to help.

Bed one: Well, there's all kinds doctors.

Bed two: Are you insinuating that my doctor . . . ?

Bed one: I wouldn't insinuate, but what is he a lefty, he sewed you up from the wrong side it takes six weeks?

Bed two: It's a complicated case.

Bed one: Well, if he's not a lefty he's a liar.

Bed two: What do you mean?

Bed one: With a gallbladder, three weeks you're home!

Education, another basic component of survival, finds the Yiddish Thinker at his most sanguine. Your high school scholar was not accepted by the college of his choice. It is a time for incorrigible optimism, Yiddish style:

"Yale turned me down."

"So? Did Christopher Columbus have to go to Yale?"

"I didn't even get my second or third choice."

"Wonderful. There's a hundred colleges begging, scream-
ing for a student like you."

"Now I'm too late to apply."

"Late isn't dead. There's cancellations."

"I'll probably have to go to some cow college."

"Marvelous. There you'll be a Phi Beta Kaplan."

"Sure, with a degree in animal husbandry."

"If you can find an animal a husband it's a nice thing, too."

"I'll get drafted first anyhow."

"They'll send you to Europe, it's like a vacation."

"They'll probably send me to Asia."

"Even in Asia the Army needs office workers."

"My luck I'll be a foot soldier."

"So you'll walk slow."

"And I'll be killed."

"And a month later they'll send me a letter, it's a mistake.
Every day I read about this in the papers!"

With a parent like this, who needs Yale?

Family background, too, is a favorite subject for Yiddish
Optimism. At the funeral of her father a few years ago, a
woman acquaintance who is in her late thirties was informed
by an aunt:

"Did you know we're from royal blood?"

"What are you saying, Auntie?" she protested.

"Absolutely. In the old country your father's people were
from the nobility."

"But that's insane," my friend said, "we're Jewish people.
There is no royalty among Jews."

"Who says? In Rumania many Jews were princes and
princesses, not kings maybe, but all the other."

My friend decided not to pursue the subject, because it
was a nice fantasy, after all. But then she could not resist the

question: "Auntie, why have you waited all these years to tell me this?"

"Darling," she explained, "it's not the kind of thing you talk about. Who would believe it?"

No chapter on Yiddish Optimism could fail to discuss its value in yet one more vital life area: romance. Every Yiddish Thinker has in him or her at least a small strain of the *shadchen* . . . the Jewish matchmaker of long ago. It is an optimism mixed with salesmanship, for even in this age of free romantic choice, the Yiddish Thinker does not entirely forget the business aspects of love. And by business I do not mean exclusively financial. For instance, you are a divorcée with three children and a house. You are pretty, available, but find it difficult to meet men. A Yiddish Thinking friend phones:

"Joyce? I have someone I'd like you to meet."

"Oh, who is it?"

"You know, Joyce, small men are very dynamic."

"He's short?"

"Did you know Napoleon was small? And Einstein?"

"How short is he?"

"They're also known to be very polite."

"Lois, I'm five foot ten."

"And they get along great with kids probably because they look like them."

"Lois, thanks but no thanks. No midgets please."

(LONG PAUSE ON OTHER END) ". . . Joyce . . . I understand. Listen, did I ever tell you about this fella Ron? A dresser like you've never seen. . . ."

I have heard this kind of dialogue only slightly exaggerated hundreds of times between friends and friends, mothers and daughters, sisters and brothers. The romance salesman is seldom effective, of course, when he works his spiel on another

Yiddish Thinker. But, the next time you observe a very short man and tall wife, or an elegantly dressed 300-pound husband on the arm of a miniature woman, or a lady of nymphlike complexion who is fifty years old escorted by a youthful Bulgarian immigrant and they all seem blissfully happy, you must believe that somehow, in some way, the Yiddish Optimist has made his influence felt.

This influence works in strange ways, indeed. Lacking a birth certificate, a middle-aged friend who was applying for a passport needed quick corroboration of his identity. It was necessary for a relative to provide an affidavit. As it happened, his only living U.S. relation was an elderly great-aunt, a real Yiddish Thinking Optimist. The following represents her filled-out questionnaire more or less as the authorities received it:

Please Answer All Questions

1. Your relation to the applicant?
   Great-Aunt.
2. Your age?
   [Erasure] 40.
3. Are you a U.S. citizen?
   [Erasure-Erasure] Absolutely.
4. Were you in attendance at the applicant's birth?
   Yes. [He is 45]
5. Is the applicant a natural-born citizen?
   Is George Washington the first President?
6. What is the applicant's place of birth?
   [Erasure] Cleveland and New Jersey.
7. To your knowledge, has the applicant ever changed his name legally?
   Yes. He's no crook.
8. Has the applicant any aliases?
   Never. Only measles and Hooping Pox.

9. Do you know of any reason why the applicant should not leave the country?

   Yes.

10. Would you explain?

    All his people in Europe are shnorers.

Signature [*Erasure*] *Joseph I. Levinsky.* [His father's name!]

When my friend later asked his great-aunt why she had signed his father's name she said, "They'll listen more to a father than to an aunt."

Not surprisingly, the affidavit was accepted, for not even the dullest bureaucrat would dare question the sincerity of such an outrageous endorsement.

7

MARTYRDOM
or
The Oy Oy Principle

"Oy oy!"

A young Gentile couple, friends of my wife from the Middle West, moved to a Jewish neighborhood in New York City. Among the many puzzling new situations the young woman encountered was her regular trip to the local market. There, inevitably, she was accosted by *yentehs*, a breed of nosy women unchallenged in all the world for the relentlessness of their pursuit.

Honey, this is your baby in the carriage?
He's white as a ghost! Try a nice vitamin.

Sweetheart, you're buying a twenty-nine-cent lettuce
when today they're on sale in the next aisle
for only fifteen?"

Darling, I think your baby needs another
blanket, he's a little blue.

Cookie, do me a favor and put back the lamb
chops. A nice piece chuck tastes just as good and
you'll have a little something left for a rainstorm.

The young mother, shy and ill equipped to deal with such
brashness, could only smile in infuriated silence. Finally, unable any longer to bear these one-way wagglers, she turned
to a friend for advice.

"Next time one of those magpies tongue-tackles you, just
tell her, 'Oh, go screw off!' You won't be bothered any more,"
said the friend.

And so at the next opportunity . . .

"Honey, do you know your baby is turning red with all
those blankets? A little fresh oxygen never killed anyone."

"Oh, go screw off!"

But perhaps you've guessed the outcome. Harsh words that
would send the hairiest sailor running back to sea have no
such effect on the Yiddish Thinker.

Those same eyes that had seemed cold and small as Roose-
velt-head dimes formed genuine tears. The same face that
had had all the tenderness of a shopping bag, now flushed and
turned soft and radiant.

"Oy, oy, darling," spoke the erstwhile tormentor. "If you only
knew. It's from loneliness that an old woman talks to you. At
home should I talk to a wall? That's what I have. A table,
darling. A wall and a table. Sure a widow has an insurance,
but can she talk to it? Care for it? In the movies you can't
talk they shush you. And you think I get even one long-
distance from my children in God-knows-where, California?"

At this rush of humility, the young wife was of course
mortified.

Martyrdom is such a common tactic of the Yiddish Thinker,
one may martyr himself three or four times before breakfast.
And, as you can see from the preceding story, no true anti-

dote for Yiddish martyrdom exists. Only another Yiddish Thinker knows how to cope with a Yiddish martyr.

My mother was once horrified to discover that my married sister did not intend to swathe her expensive new furniture in protective plastic coverings.

This brought on the whole doleful story of her life without means and the many hardships that led her to respect an unsoiled down-and-spring cushion and a fine-nubbed silken fabric untouched by human trousers. At last, her emotions spent, she was able forlornly to choke out the inevitable question: "Oy, and what will you do with this gorgeous furniture when, one year from now, it's all dirty and *bakockt?*"

My brother-in-law, a good Yiddish Thinker, had the only answer. "When that happens, Mom," he said, "I'm going to throw it all out in the alley!"

But martyrdom can be a very useful, if selfish, ingredient of Yiddish Thinking. This, more or less, is how it works. The Yiddish Thinker knows that for most of us life is, at best, a drab affair. Rich or poor, few of us become celebrities or are recognized by history. Our lives count for little even in the estimation of our closest friends and family. Thus we must dramatize our lives to others, but especially to ourselves. And the essential element of drama is tragedy. A Yiddish Thinker can shape a tragedy out of almost anything. A toothache, a missed airplane, post-nasal drip. A friend who spent some time in his early life as a shoe clerk found among prosperous female Yiddish Thinkers what may be one of the most common excuses for martyrdom: the hard-to-fit foot. The idea prevalent among these women was to experience— or imagine experiencing—the worst possible hardships in locating a shoe suitable for the unusual contours of their feet. Learning that the goal of these women was really to be unsuccessful in the purchase of a pair of shoes in order to enhance their martyrdom in the eyes of their pals, my friend decided one day to see just how far they would go.

"That camel suede pump in the window? Would you have it in purple?"

"Yes, indeed," my friend lied.

"Oh? But I really require a higher heel," said the shopper.

"In that case, we have it," said my friend.

"With a platform sole is really what I'm looking for, however," said she.

"That too we have," said he, piling lie upon lie.

"Well, I don't suppose you'd carry my size in that style," she persisted, "a ten quint A?"

"I'll bring it right out."

". . . but with a seven A heel?"

"Absolutely. I've got just the shoe."

"But wait!" she said with some panic (as if by now he had to be told). ". . . Uh, come to think of it I really don't care for that yellow sock lining."

"Pink, green, orange, whatever color you want in a sock lining, we've got it, lady." He looked her straight in the eye.

"Mauve?"

"Mauve!"

Without so much as a blink of remorse, the non-customer turned, said she'd come back tomorrow and, of course, did not. I can see the lady now, basking in her foot martyrdom, boasting to friends, ". . . You know what they tell me in the stores? 'With a foot like yours, madame, to get any kind of styling, you have to go to a custom shoemaker.' Oy, oy, girls, to have a shoe custom-made, do you realize what this costs . . . ?"

And another of them is saying, "Hah! My chiropodist tells me with a foot like mine I shouldn't even be wearing shoes!"

Time for another old joke. (Some say all ethnic jokes are the same; adaptable by merely exchanging one dialect for another. I wonder. Try and imagine this one as, say, an Italian joke.)

Jewish couple in Pullman car. She in the top berth, he below. For nearly two hours during the hot night he has listened to her complaining from above:

"Oy, am I toisty. Oy, am I toisty."

She's thirsty, he mutters, and I can't sleep because of it. So he scrambles from bed and fetches her a glass of water.

She drinks gratefully. He rearranges himself in his berth. There is a brief silence. He is just about to doze off, when he hears:

"Oy, *was* I toisty! Oy, was I toisty!"

It is wrong, in Yiddish Thinking, to give the appearance that life is easy for you, even if it is. This notion is, no doubt, of superstitious origin, going back to a time when no Jew would tempt fate by saying things were well in a Gentile world which could at any moment take a turn for the worse.

You may have noticed an interesting point of style among Yiddish martyrs. They create tragedies as though lighting matches—instantaneously. The expert martyr has no use for preliminaries. To construct a tragedy painstakingly is all right for a Shakespeare. It only grants time, however, in which the experienced Yiddish Thinking listener may guess the motive and slide into disbelief. No, the good Yiddish martyr enters in a panic and sustains that pitch to the end.

I know a very soft-hearted woman who was, for most of her life, at the mercy of a hard-up sister who used the telephone as an instrument of tragedy.

Rrrrring! "Frieda? Nola. My boy just had his eyes checked and they're sending him to a blind school it's so bad. A blind school! Oy, oy!" Click.

Translation: I need fifteen bucks to buy the kid a pair of glasses.

Rrring! "Frieda? Nola. Oy! Oy! I've just arrived at the

hospital and they're amputating my leg in a minute, I fell down the stairs coming home from my night job, how would you know, a housewife who never had to work?" Click.

Translation: I'm home with a sprained ankle. How about taking care of the kids this evening.

Rrring! "Frieda? Nola. Irv [her husband] is in jail. Murdered a police officer. Oy! Oy! We're not all so fortunate to have married a law-abiding genius husband." Click.

Translation: Could you loan Irv twenty bucks to pay a speeding ticket?

Rrring! "Frieda? Nola. Please inform the family that I am taking my life in five minutes. With iodine!" Click!

Translation: Oy! Oy!

Yiddish martyrdom, for all its conceit, can bring about a highly successful *modus vivendi* among friends and particularly within families.

One family I know has three brothers whose martyrdoms perfectly complement each other. Let us call them Bernie, Moe and Max. Bernie, the successful brother, owns a thriving hotel, which is managed for him by brother Moe. Max, a miser, and the least successful brother, has arranged with Bernie to occupy space rent-free in the hotel for operating his own small business. Max is a hard-luck martyr. He never made it big like Bernie because he never had the "breaks." Moe is a work martyr. If it weren't for his diligence and loyalty, Bernie's hotel would go bust. Bernie is a noblesse oblige martyr, who, by virtue of his success, sees himself as the long-suffering protector of his kin.

In arranging for use of the free office space, Max naturally had to bypass Moe, whose obsessive business efficiency could not tolerate such an indulgence.

To Bernie, however, this was an opportunity to dispense favors with a magnanimity God would expect of few men but himself. So, without Moe's knowledge, Bernie agreed to pay Max $100 a month. Max in turn then would write a check for $100, handing it over each month to Bernie's agent, brother Moe.

To this day, on the last Thursday of each month, Max, in the presence of brother Moe, writes his check with a proud flourish and the complaint: "Oy! A rich brother takes from a poor brother $100 every month, it's okay a person who never had any luck doesn't ask for a break." Brother Moe receives the check and reports, "Every month the miser pays like the rest. Oy! Oy! I see to that or you'd be out of business tomorrow." Brother Bernie, meanwhile, who might just as easily have given the space free in the first place, confides to me of the rigmarole he must go through just to "keep peace in the family, oy oy oy!"

Perhaps it has occurred to you already how you may put martyrdom Yiddish Style to work for you in your everyday life. If you spot your opportunities, it can be at best useful, and at the least, fun.

For example, you are being pestered by life insurance salesmen. You have tried all the usual rebuffs, but there is no getting rid of them. You martyr yourself:

"Oy, buddy, you're right. If anybody should have more life insurance it's me. Sure the doc says it's hemorrhoids. But I know different. Hemorrhoids in the armpit? In the throat? The policies I have already, all dog-eared, laying around the house like a public library. The *kids* read them, the *momsers*. But I don't complain. I'm not sensitive. I see the brochures from the mortuary, she keeps them next to the car payments. And suddenly she's pushing cigarettes in my mouth. Insurance? Absolutely. I'll take $500,000 of your best. Can you make it over here in a half-hour? Surgery day today, you know."

Most of your friends are college graduates and you barely made it through high school? Become an education martyr:

"You heard of the School of Hard Knocks? That's in the Ivy League compared to where *I* went to college. Crapover U. That's *my* old tomato. Why, with my family I had as much chance of becoming a freshman as Christine Jorgensen becoming a mother. Pa was a used organ-grinder salesman. Ma sewed parachutes for the Italian marines. I was the oldest of fourteen children including three sets of Siamese twins, and every one of them was an invalid. I was such a hardship case I applied to the Army as a Conscientious Approver! But you don't hear me knocking eduation. Not me. I used to dream of those college courses. The names were fascinating. Rhetoric! Remedial Math! Pharmacology! And I'd have been one helluva Remedial Mathematician given half a chance. Ah well, as they say, higher education isn't for the masses, which I'm one of—I guess—although I'm not a Catholic. Anyway, good luck with your Ph.D.'s and your B.S.'s and your M.A.'s I think it's marvelous that you never had even one invalid to support, not that I wish it on anybody. Oy! Oy!"

If that sounds a little like your favorite comedian's monologue, it's no coincidence. Many of today's most popular comics—Jackie Vernon, Joan Rivers, Rodney Dangerfield, Phil Foster—to name a few, have built fabulous careers on the simple Yiddish martyr story.

If public issues were approached from the point of view of the Yiddish martyr, that is, if we could produce guilt on a scale that would infiltrate the federal bureaucracy or the unfeeling giant corporations, think of the progress we could make.

Consumerism

President, Amalgamated Motors
Detroit, Michigan
Dear Sonny boy,
Some cars you make now. An $8,000 car the door comes

off in your hand. People everywhere, you see them walking around with doors in their hands. Cheapos! What do you care? People riding around in cars with no doors falling out on their heads. Shame on you. And the paint? What is that, watercolors it peels off in two days? It's probably the kind with the lead in it that the babies are eating, everyday you hear about it the poor babies are croaking. With the poison gas coming out of the tailpipe, everybody's crying, choking in the streets. You probably never drive yourself, flying around in airplanes. 757's. Making more poison smoke even. It's okay. It's all right. Don't do nothing about it. Go. Fly. Let the people figure it out. Oy, oy.

God bless you,
You know who

Women's Liberation

President, United States of America
Washington, D.C.
Dear Sonny boy,
What do you know about a woman? By you it's a doll, you want to shnoogle it. It doesn't matter to you a woman breaks her back all her life for you, never complains. She wears garments with rubber in it making lines, cutting the blood off from her body for who? For her? For you! She should look like a doll. Oy, it's a man's world. And don't tell me about your First Lady either. She stands in the shadows giving a little smile—a mouse smile—while you're making big speeches it's going to help the country. Phooey! What do you pay her, hah? What's her salary, booby? I'll tell you. A kiss. Hundred million women living on a kiss. A man, a *shlemiel*, gets fifty dollars an hour now. What do you pay a woman? "Here's a little something, honey, go get your hair done and I'll give you a smooch." Thank

you very much. Anything you can do it's appreciated. Only one suggestion. How about with the scientific technology they figure out how the man can have the baby? Nice, hah? Just something you'll think about while you're playing golf, hah? Sorry to bother you with such small things, it's just that the heat got to me a little bit today in the kitchen.

Love and kisses,
What'shername

Campus Disorders

President, Students for a Just Society
Yoyo University
Dear Sonny boy,
So now you're a bomber, hah? Where did you learn this, from Hitler? I know, I know. It's only a building. So come home you'll blow up our house for practice. Wonderful. Believe me, us establishmentniks know exactly how you feel. We take all the blame. Oy oy! It's our fault we went personally to Viet Nam and said, "Please, we beg you let's have a war." Because we're what they call "racists," we can't stand any colored people, only the children of your generation like them. Never before, nobody liked colored people until you came along. Also, we invented the atomic bomb, all of us. The man next-door invented one in his kitchen. We invented ours—as you know—one day on our summer vacation. So, if you're making just little bombs, who can blame you? We failed you, us establishmentniks, where I don't know?

Well, just thought I'd drop a note before I went out for a little afternoon genocide. Don't bother to write.

Fondly,
Someone whose name you wouldn't remember

"You can fight city hall, but fight nice."—Mayer Deli

8

THE YIDDISH-GOYISH VALUE GAP
or
Sterility Shmerility

There is one last adjustment to make before you can really begin to Think Yiddish. You must do some fiddling with the fine tuner on your set of values. Although I have said the Yiddish Thinker ignores distinctions and scorns aesthetics, no thought system could function without some elementary scale of values. Yiddish values are no less important because they are loosely defined and freely interpreted. In fact, their usefulness becomes apparent when they are compared with values which are "non-Yiddish."

The late comedian Lenny Bruce invented an intriguing exercise to distinguish what is "Yiddish" or Jewish from what is "Goyish" or Gentile. He quite properly pointed out that since Yiddish is not a literal language it can use the word "Goyish" to mean even Jews. At the same time, "Yiddish" may describe non-Jews.

For instance, anybody who lives in a big city, according to Bruce, is Yiddish, even if he's a Catholic. On the other hand, if you live in Butte, Montana, to use his example, you're

"Goyish" even if you're Yiddish. This reasoning applies to all people, places and things. It's a bit like the game of "In" and "Out," except what's in isn't always so terrific, and what's out isn't always so terrible.

Consider the sixty-year-old Yiddish Thinking man of my acquaintance who, faced with a hernia operation, was warned by the surgeon that certain complications of his case might call for the removal of a testicle.

"No, absolutely," exclaimed the YT.

"In that case," the doctor cautioned, "you should know that you run the risk of sterility."

"Sterility shmerility," said the Thinker, "I'll take symmetry."

For a sixty-year-old male, sterility is Goyish; symmetry, as my friend put it so alliteratively, is Yiddish.

Business is, of course, Yiddish. But the various ways of conducting business may be either Yiddish or Goyish. One of the most successful salesmen I know traveled exclusively by train, in sleeper cars. They were his luxury, his haven, the thing that made his many difficult years on the road tolerable, worthwhile. Once, destined for Cleveland, he was told by the ticket clerk that no sleeper accommodations were available.

"Very well," he said, "I'll take a sleeper to Des Moines."

"Sorry," said the clerk, "nothing to Des Moines."

"Okay," said the super salesman, never batting an eyelash, "then put me on a sleeper to Buffalo."

Once again, the clerk checked over his lists. And once more, almost happily it seemed, he shook his head. "No dice, sir. No sleepers available to Buffalo, either."

But there was no stopping him. "Okay, pal," said the salesman, "then give me a nice sleeper to Louisville."

The clerk could no longer contain his contempt. "Sir," he said, "if you don't mind my saying so, I think that's a hell of a way to run a business."

"And *that*, sonny," said the salesman, "is why *you're* taking tickets and *I'm* taking sleepers!"

The next day, a very well-rested super salesman wrote a magnificent order in Terre Haute.

Some further examples will help to increase your Power of Yiddish Thinking. Commit these to memory and thereafter you should be able to make Yiddish value judgments without any hesitation (the Yiddish Thinker never hesitates):

Tweed is GOYISH	Shantung is YIDDISH
Hunting is GOYISH	Sunbathing is YIDDISH
Richard Nixon is GOYISH	Ronald Reagan is YIDDISH
Fireplaces are GOYISH	Air Conditioning is YIDDISH
Alaska is GOYISH	Hawaii is YIDDISH
Dawn is GOYISH	Noon is YIDDISH
Sex is GOYISH	Dating is YIDDISH
Motels are GOYISH	Hotels are YIDDISH
Football is GOYISH	Football tickets are YIDDISH
Miniskirts are GOYISH	Cleavage is YIDDISH
Firemen are GOYISH	Cabdrivers are YIDDISH
Gout is GOYISH	Ulcers are YIDDISH
Cafeterias are GOYISH	Chinese food is YIDDISH
Chiropodists are GOYISH	Dentists are YIDDISH

Generally speaking, what is "Yiddish" by this definition is: new, easy, comfortable, safe, voluptuous, exotic, clean, glamorous and expensive. What is "Goyish" is: rugged, dangerous, inconvenient, messy, plain, old and necessary. Obviously, there are contradictions in the above list, but in these cases one value merely takes precedence over another. For example, motels are more convenient than hotels, but glamor is more important than convenience. Dawn is more glamorous than

noon, but convenience, in this instance, is more important
than glamor. The single most Yiddish thing in the world is,
I think, color TV. For the least Yiddish, a good guess would
by Reykjavik, Iceland.

A good example of one Yiddish value having priority over
another occurs every year at Christmastime. Christmas itself is, of course, very Yiddish. But when you break Christmas
down into its components, well that's another matter altogether. For example, expensive is Yiddish, and so is generosity,
but . . . A $200 gift certificate is Yiddish. Five hundred dol-
lars worth of presents is Goyish. Vacations are Yiddish and so
is entertaining but . . . Miami in season is Yiddish; caroling
in the streets is Goyish. Both social obligations and interior
decorating are Yiddish, but . . . Christmas cards are Yiddish;
Christmas trees are Goyish. And so on and on. In Christmas,
of all things, one can find an almost complete range of Yiddish
values at their most versatile.

But let me illustrate a very typical conflict of Yiddish values,
so that you may understand not only the priorities but the
dynamics which establish these priorities. Family, for example,
is an important Yiddish value. So is money. The Yiddish
Thinker places a high value on close family associations and
dependencies. At the same time, he has no less regard for the
importance of cash dollars. As a youth, a friend of mine was
sent off to his uncle's clothing store in the expectation of re-
ceiving the most special consideration on the price of a new
suit of clothes.

Since no garment in the shop was marked by price, but
only by code, my friend—being a good Yiddish Thinker, even
at his age—was quick to determine both the actual cost and
the minimum acceptable profit for each item. He had
cracked the code.

Selecting a suit he calculated at a cost of thirty dollars, he
presented it to his relative.

"For you," said the uncle, "fifty dollars."

"But, uncle," said the young upstart, "I happen to know that you sell this same suit to your ordinary customers for only forty dollars. How can you ask fifty dollars from your own flesh and blood?"

"Nu," said the uncle, wise as the hills in the ways of Yiddish Thinking, "so if I can't make a living off of my own flesh and blood, who can I make it off of?"

A clear-cut victory for money over family, or is it family over money?

Yiddish values not only vary in priority, they are flexible as well to the demands of changing times. They may be adapted from century to century, from year to year, or even from minute to minute. Consider this conversation between two fathers on the sideline of a Little League baseball game:

Dad #1:   That your boy at bat?

Dad #2:   Uh huh.

Dad #1:   How's he doing?

Dad #2:   He was leading hitter last year.

Dad #1:   For the whole team?

Dad #2:   For the whole league. Worldwide.

Dad #1:   An upcoming Mickey Mantle, huh?

Dad #2:   We think so. Baseball's in his blood. Which is yours?

Dad #1:   He's the pitcher.

Dad #2:   What's his record?

Dad #1:   27 and 0. He's pitched eleven straight no-hitters. Major league scouts have been inquiring already.

Dad #2:   Lots of strikeouts, huh?

Dad #1:   Yep. There's strike one.

Dad #2:   They say all that throwing makes them cripples.

Dad #1:   Oops, there's strike two.

Dad ♯2: We've felt for some time that these competitive sports are overemphasized at this early age.

Dad ♯1: Ohh, too bad. Your boy struck out.

Dad ♯2: He's really made up his mind to be a surgeon, feels that baseball, after all, is just a silly game.

Dad ♯1: Well, be seein' ya. Fire it in there, Johnny!

Dad ♯2: Sure. Who knows? Maybe someday your boy will be coming to my boy for work on that crippled elbow. 'Bye now.

One of the most basic Goyish values, the family name, provides a fascinating example of the adaptable Yiddish value. It is a comment on the Yiddish Thinker's contempt for names that my own family name, Marcus, was given to my immigrant grandfather in exchange for some Polish monicker which today, only two generations later, no member of my family can even recall. In Yiddish Thinking, one may change his name as he changes his tie. There are no Rockefellers or Cabot-Lodges among Yiddish Thinkers.

The grandfather of a friend of mine appeared on these shores bearing the unlikely name (for a Jew) of Beldover. Knowing that to make his way in his new country he must begin, at least, among his fellow Jews, he immediately changed his name to Goldstein. And Goldstein the family name remained until his son, settling into an occupation which associated him about half and half with Jews and Gentiles, felt the need for a name of more ambiguous connotations. Something half and half. Not Beldover certainly. And not Goldstein. So he called himself Stein. I have asked my friend if he has ever considered going back to Beldover. "No, I still consider that a bit much," he says, "and anyway, for where we live now and for my business, we're very happy with Stone."

Speaking of names, the simplest application of Yiddish values I have ever observed was my late good friend Harry's habit of dubbing all of his favorite celebrities with Jewish monickers. The world's most beautiful women, he insisted, were Jewish. Agnes Moorehead was Alice Wertheimer. Greta Garbo was Gertrude Graubart. Sonja Henie became Sandra Hyman. And Carmen Miranda was the Jewish Latin Bombshell Connie Mandel.

The great men of his day, in recognition of their brains, good looks or accomplishments were assigned more familiar Jewish names. Knute Rockne was Nate Rotstein. Colin Kelly was Kalman Cohen. F. Scott Fitzgerald was really Gerald F. Katzman. And Douglas Fairbanks was, of course, that dashing Jewish cavalier David Farber, Jr.

Yiddish values, let's make it clear, have nothing whatever to do with moral judgments. If you wish, for example, to go hunting with a lot of firemen and stay at a motel in Reykjavik, the Yiddish Thinker might think you a bit whifty, but never would he disapprove. For, above all, the Yiddish Thinker respects *shtick*. *Shtick* is what has become known, particularly in the jargon of youth, as "doing one's thing." Whether it be Yiddish or Goyish, everyone has a shtick, and shtick is shtick.

It is only when a person violates his own shtick that a Yiddish Thinker complains. For instance, if Spiro Agnew (Goyish) were suddenly to throw all his support to the Southern Christian Leadership Conference (Yiddish), he would be dismissed as an erratic and untrustworthy public figure. Mr. Agnew is, after all, most familiar for his law-and-order shtick. He is fond of patient, courteous citizens and he can't stand a lot of hollering and carrying on in the streets. It means nothing that such a shift might have come from a sincere change of heart or that you, yourself, sympathize with the aims and practices of this organization. In response to this kind of development, the Yiddish Thinker thinks:

"So where does a Spiro Agnew come to a Ralph Abernathy?"

To the Yiddish Thinker, a person returns from the dead easier than he changes his shtick.

That the Pope (Goyish) did not soften his position on birth control (Yiddish) is perfectly understandable to the Yiddish Thinker. On the other hand, that the overpopulated Catholics (Yiddish) should take the Pope's instructions seriously would be utterly and inexplicably Goyish.

If the mayor (Goyish) of Chicago (Yiddish) had welcomed the protesters (Goyish) instead of siccing the police on them (Goyish), maybe that riot (Goyish) would have turned out to be just a *tzimmis* (Yiddish). The real problem, of course, was that many of the demonstrators were not Goyish and some of the policemen were Yiddish. It was a case of shtick-betrayal on a mass scale. Thus, as any Yiddish Thinking astrologist could tell you, the result was written in the shticks.

Now that you have a grasp of Yiddish values, take a good Yiddish look at yourself. Maybe you're a black lady (Yiddish) who would like to live her life as a blonde (Yiddish). Go ahead! Don't listen to those black panthers (Goyish). You're a social bridge player (Goyish) in a penny-a-point game (Yiddish)? Get out while you still have your socks! Or maybe your daughter has eloped (Goyish) when you were planning an expensive wedding (Yiddish). Don't give them any money (Yiddish). Go have yourself a bash (Goyish) in some place like Las Vegas (Yiddish).

"That's the customer we call 'Marcia of the Mountains,'
because of her Grand Tetons."—Cousin Vera

9

A CASE STUDY
or
Portrait of the YT as a Middle-aged Cousin

We have now arrived at a point where nothing may serve
you quite so well as what the social scientists call a "role
model." A case study of the archetypal Yiddish Thinker in
action. And for this, I can do you no better than to reveal
my own role model. My inspiration, my mentor, my beau
ideal of a Yiddish Thinker. My cousin Vera.

Vera is not perfect. There is no more a perfect Yiddish
Thinker than there is a perfect swimmer or a perfect hair-
dresser. Vera is deficient, for example, as a martyr. She is
exceptionally gifted in chutzpah, can trade Flat Statements
with the best, and has a deadly acumen with the Big Putdown. She is so strong in these other departments that she
tends to be unconvincing in the martyr's hair shirt.

Cousin Vera's values, however, are solid. At her son's wedding dinner, the speeches and the toasts were going on and
on and on, when she noticed a ruby-red glow around the
young man's neck.

With his well-packed bride at his side, perspiration hung about his ears, his eyes bulged and black whiskers were already sprouting through his face powder.

She knew he had still to endure a long auto ride to the airport, several hours on the plane and yet more of the business of travel before finally reaching the isolation of his honeymoon bed.

And still the toasts went on:

"To Larry and his Myra, may the days be as flowers in the bower of their life together."

"To the gorgeous groom and his delicious bride. They should only bring into this world children so handsome and well-shaped and nice-mannered as themselves."

"To the new Mister and Missus America. . . ."

At this point, Vera leaned over to me and said quite audibly, "For Christ's sake. If these *momsers* don't shut up soon, the kid's so horny he's liable to rape her in the phone booth at the airport altogether!" The festivities ended very shortly afterward.

Earlier at this same wedding, when it was learned that the hosts had ordered the bar closed after dinner, Cousin Vera, who wears flowered hats and speaks, by the way, in the most genteel and lady-like tone of voice, was overheard to say, "Well, F—— them!"

But this woman, who once said of her post-pubic daughter's pediatrician, "He keeps the panties down a little too long to suit me," is a Yiddish Thinker far beyond the ability to put the mean and the fatuous swiftly down to earth.

Let us see Truth—Yiddish Truth—through the eyes of a nonpareil Yiddish Thinker, Cousin Vera. On Fashion (Vera owns a dress shop):

"The midi length looks like horsedung on most women. They are now using deformed models to show off these dresses. Girls with no rib cage, the waist right under the neck and legs that look like flagpoles, because some fairies in France want normal women to look like communists. You wait and see, babushkas and shopping bags are the next high-fashion articles and heavy coats made out of rope and fake gold teeth. And canes. And yellow anklets. . . . But on you, Mrs. Fagelson, I think this look is nice."

Cousin Vera on money:

"You take your money today and spend it or wipe with it. Only a *shmuck* saves it today. Save dead leaves better. Old magazines. Save chicken fat. A hundred-dollar bill today isn't worth a piece of snot. My sister-in-law is saving, putting it in the bank, meanwhile she's living like a pilgrim, eating tea and buns in a rocking chair getting gray hair and eyestrain watching the electric bills. And her husband, my brother, is giving himself haircuts and buying regular gas. Meanwhile, in Washington they're printing five hundred billion dollars a day to buy a new gun or a bomb to blow up some Chinamen and the inflation goes up and up and the money in the bank is in the toilet! Plunk down your money. Flush! Every week, the paycheck, plunk! flush! That's right, cousin. Banks today are toilets and people who save in them have terminal diarrhea!"

Vera on the Family:

"Anything beyond a first cousin in the house is a disease. A family is a father, a mother, a son, a daughter, a niece, a nephew, a cousin, and after that it's a *momser*. A son? He'll marry an Eskimo, a pygmy, a circus act, what's the difference what *you* think? A daughter will run off with the grocer, she'll jump on the elevator man, what's it to you? An in-law is a wart that grows on you later in life, it doesn't go away so you wash it and treat it like the rest of your body. But a second cousin! A second cousin is a *goniff!* You see him three times in your whole life and he asks if he can borrow $50,000. He lives in Texas, in Minneapolis, Godknowswhere, laughing at you, peeing on you to his friends and neighbors. And for your daughter's wedding he sends an alarm clock from the dime store with a bar mitzvah card. He's someone who made a million dollars prewar and stuffed it in a shoe, in his nose, I don't know, but would cross to the other side if he saw you selling matches on a street corner."

"And how then should *your* second cousins feel about *you?*" I once asked her.

She answered, "They should kiss my feet that I don't think that way about them."

But Cousin Vera would never be the consummate Thinker that she is without her superlative gift of chutzpah.

Several years ago, Vera moved with her family into a conservative new development of small tidy ranch houses. Straight streets, rectangular blocks, neatly trimmed front and back yards, all the homes facing the street on fifty-foot lots looking pretty much the same. Her first act was to rip out the front yard and install a circular driveway!

"Good grief! For heaven's sake! What the hell?" said the neighbors, as their cars, in awed procession, cruised by for days afterward.

Abashed by this reaction, Vera delayed at least three weeks before opening her dress and corset shop in the basement. For months, the clientele streamed in through the kitchen while the neighborly gossip just streamed.

Success brought Vera out of her basement at last, and, somehow, during the neighbors sleep or something, but narrowly within the zoning laws, a huge new commercial building was being raised on a nearby corner carrying the name of Vera in huge letters across the front.

"Good God! Is she mad? Is it legal? Is it even moral?" The neighbors were dumbfounded. Vera only smiled and said, "*Vehr geharget*" behind her teeth.

Business boomed down at the corner and it was not long

before the workmen came to tear out the back yard for the installation of the pool.

"A pool? In this neighborhood?" The neighbors were right. No one in charge of his senses would dream of a real down-in-the-ground pool adjoining a six-room ranch house.

The pool, a lulu, consumed almost the entire width and length of Vera's back yard, leaving enough space only for a phalanx of cabanas at the rear.

"CABANAS? I'M DYING!"

Yes, cabanas, and very smart ones at that. And a high diving board. And a deck. And, finally, of course, a sliding dome and a boardwalk. And the crowning irony, well known to all the neighbors, was that neither Vera nor any member of her family knew how to swim!

Thus it came as no surprise when, later, Vera began re-building her house itself from top to bottom . . . tearing out walls here, adding rooms there; creating sunken bathrooms and elevated dining areas until ultimately every usable inch of that fifty-foot lot was crammed with the products of Vera's brazen imagination. Today, one can only appreciate Vera's accomplishment by circling slowly overhead in a helicopter. There, in a perfect rectangle of conventional homes rises a palace, a carnival—no, a glittering monument to one woman's chutzpah.

Non-conformism, you say? In a way, but so much more. The neighbor's final solace was, of course, that Vera would never get her investment back. But it was Pyrrhic, for they knew equally well that she never intended to leave.

Creatures of chutzpah, as I have shown earlier, never lose, for to lose implies an acknowledgment of defeat, and the word is not in their vocabulary.

More chutzpah from Cousin Vera. But to understand its significance, we must first re-examine some Yiddish Values.

Skiing is Goyish. After all, it involves snow and cold and

potential injury. Therefore, Cousin Vera does not ski, nor does anyone she knows.

Ah, but the romance, the ambience of skiing is quite another thing. Moonlight on snowscapes! Hot toddies around the fire! Lessons from glamorous Europeans! Pinochle in the lodge! Why, everything about skiing is Yiddish after all, except the skiing.

And so Vera set out for a ski holiday. To ensure the success of it she naturally took along eight non-skiing friends and relations, all accomplished pinochle players and lounge lizards. But a very Goyish thing happened along the way to Vera and her party. A northern blizzard halted their train somewhere in the wilds of Michigan. What to do in a country town with no hotel and nine frozen *tochases* loaded down with enough luggage for twenty?

A farmhouse. A light in the window. A knock on the door. A farmer with a lamp. What else?

Vera peered around the startled farmer for a view inside. A table prepared with old foods like meat and bread and porridge as opposed to New York strips, egg rolls and minestrone. And not one jello mold in sight! A smell of lard. A New Testament on the sideboard. Probably the most un-Yiddish scene her eyes had ever focused upon.

Though Vera paused here not even for a moment, we must, to analyze yet another question of values. Strict religious devotion is Goyish. It is associated with austerity, abstinence and frugality, all valid, but nevertheless foreign in concept to the Yiddish Thinker. (Orthodox Judaism is Goyish.) Thus Cousin Vera and almost everybody she knows has an ad-lib arrangement with the Almighty. Food and shelter of any kind is far more Yiddish than religious affiliation of any kind is Goyish.

"Who be you?" said the farmer.

"We be pilgrims," said Vera.

"Pilgrims? Of what faith then?"

"We're Catholic . . . ah . . . Baptists. Catholic Baptist *Mishugenehs*. It's a . . . um . . . rare sect."

"And those?" The farmer pointed to the skis.

"Our ritual. We pray on skis. You see, we were on our way to this retreat, when . . ."

Well, it went roughly like that, and before you could say "Apostasy" Cousin Vera and eight people with names like Sharon and Karen and Brucie and Erwin were sharing bread and shelter with the most fascinated fundamentalist couple north of Reed City.

But remember, there is Love in the Yiddish Thinker, too. The picture I have painted of Cousin Vera may be, I fear, too heavy with the colors of remorselessness and expedience. It is required of a Yiddish Thinker to have absolute tolerance; the business of shticks, if you recall. And this total tolerance of differences implies a kind of love which may be nobler than the more commonplace definitions we give that emotion.

One of my favorite Cousin Vera stories concerns her love and devotion to a thief! Vera dearly loved her housekeeper, an older woman of meager education and deeply superstitious nature. The simple woman was particularly unsettled by any mention of death, ghosts, spirits and such.

One day, her housekeeper stole Cousin Vera's dentures, upper and lower plates. Or, at least, she appeared to have snatched them, for they were not in the glass tumbler on the mantel where Vera kept them. Also, the woman had been saying for months how badly she needed a pair of her own.

No question about the evidence, but how to keep her dear friend and housekeeper and still recover this indispensable possession?

"You never knew my brother, did you?" said Vera.

"Never knew you had a brother," said the housekeeper.

"Very close until the minute he died," Vera said.

The housekeeper started. "Kitchen needs sweepin'," she said.

"We were alone when his life ended. . . ."

"Ooh, don't tell me that." The housekeeper began to whistle, wiping already wiped places with a rag.

"That's when he made me promise . . ." said Vera in pursuit.

"Yankee Doodle," whistled the housekeeper, swiping frantically at invisible dustbunnies.

". . . about his teeth!"

"Eeeyah! Eeeyah!"

"That's right. They were his teeth, and I said I'd always wear them, and now they're missing."

"Aghpht! Keekeekeekyeek!"

Next morning, the family teeth were back in their glass sarcophagus, and Vera still had a friend and housekeeper.

"A person who respects the dead," says Vera (who, of course, never had a brother with or without teeth), "cannot also be a thief."

Shtick is shtick.

As for Vera's Yiddish Optimism, examples abound in her role of local fashion arbiter.

Customer: Vera, what do you think of this dress on me?

Vera: Gorgeous. It does something for your shoulder blades. Your best feature.

Customer: But purple! Tsk. Tsk. I look like a corpse in this color.

Vera: Sleeping beauty was also a corpse.

Customer: And with my small bust to wear such a low neckline?

Vera: *Shmuck.* If you only knew the number of elephants who come in here who would like to have your little marshmallows.

Customer: And a skirt so short with my veins?

Vera: At least the color matches.

Customer: But the see-through blouse! Really, Vera, I think that's too much.

Vera: Who's going to look?

Next Customer: I'm looking for something in a fuchsia or burgundy stretch knit.

Vera: Then you're a cuckoo. Or else you're planning major surgery on your behind.

Customer: I know I'm hippy, but . . .

Vera: A hippo like you walks out of here in a knit dress and they'll throw peanuts in your mouth. Honey, why hurt yourself, try a nice tailored gray suit.

Customer: I'm sick of nice tailored gray suits.

Vera: They come in brown, too.

Customer: Suits are so mannish looking.

Vera: Better to be mistaken for a man than a soft piano.

Customer: What man is going to ask me to go dancing in a tailored suit?

Vera: You'll wear extra perfume, longer nails, you'll bat your eyelashes a little more, it'll make up. What does a man know? But, please, no knits on you.

Customer: That's all I have are suits suits suits!

Vera: So? Eleanor Roosevelt wore nothing but suits and she did all right by herself.

Customer: But she was homely!

Vera: Then, cookie, try to imagine her in a fuchsia stretch knit!

If beings from another world ever show up on earth, I personally hope that instead of seeking our leaders, they make straight for some of our better Yiddish Thinkers. Cousin Vera would do just fine:

Them: We come from a distant planet.

Vera: [Big Putdown.] I could tell you're not from Staten Island.

Them: We are tired from our long journey.

Vera: You look a little green. Have some chicken soup.

Them: We *are* green.

Vera: A nice shade, however.

Them: You do not find us unsightly?

Vera: [Question/Answer.] Have you seen my cousin Lester?

Them: We are able to read your thoughts.

Vera: Congratulations. I have a nephew who can read Portuguese.

Them: We are concerned about your world's extraterrestrial ambitions.

Vera: Believe me, we wouldn't bother you. Who could live by you with craters and all that dust?

Them: Nevertheless, we come to warn you and all other earthlings.

Vera: [Flat Statement.] Where we're not wanted we wouldn't go, except maybe for the colored which you can't blame them.

Them: Only remember it is within our power to destroy your earth if we so choose.

Vera: [Megilla.] I don't know what for you're getting so excited. We've had a couple of kids up there zipping around, telling jokes in the sky. Everybody was so brave, praying, crying they should land safely in a *cockamehmeh* parachute. [Martyrdom.] Oy, oy, a billion dollars a second it's costing us for a picture postcard of the earth. Marvelous, it looks blue with white clouds, a moron knows it. And here you are dropping in for a weekend from God knows where, getting green in the face—you say it's your natural color—worried *we're* going to move into *your* neighborhood. [Yiddish Optimism.] I only wish I had your troubles. If I did, I'd take them to wherever you go for a suntan and relax for about ten million years, I still say it wouldn't hurt your complexion!

This kind of encounter could send an extraterrestrial being home questioning his superior intelligence!

> *"Never change horseradishes in the middle of a gefilte fish."*—R. Eisenberg

10

YIDDISH UPMANSHIP
or
Earning the Borscht Belt

An old friend swears that, as a youth, his Yiddish Thinking father gave him this advice: "Open your mouth, sonny, or they'll crap all over you!" Although the consequences of such a suggestion are literally repulsive, the father's meaning is quite clear. And now, knowing what you know of Yiddish Thinking, it is time for you to open your mouth, as it were. The notion of Upmanship is, of course, more properly associated with Stephen Potter's designing Englishmen and other urbane citizens of the world. Upmanship is really a gentleman's game, and to play it with Yiddish is a bit like playing field hockey with machetes. Still, as the famous showman-druggist P. T. Barnbaum recently said, "There's a *momser* born every minute." British-style upmanship may win you points at a lawn party, but if current trends continue, chances are, the next time you find yourself on the grass, it will be as the victim of a mugger in the park. For this, you need quick moves, not manners. You need mental sneakers. Verbal Karate. In short, Yiddish Upmanship.

(Although I have made a point of explaining that a Yiddish vocabulary is not required in order to use and enjoy the Power of Yiddish Thinking, in the special arena of Upmanship, a sprinkling of Yiddish words is desirable to add spice and flavor. They serve much the same purpose as horseradish on a gefilte fish.)

Verbal Karate: Beginner's Level
(Proficiency Award—The Mink Belt)

Lesson One: The Law

Motorcycle cop: Okay, buddy, pull over to the curb.

You: [It's your fourth moving violation.] Officer, did you see the man come out of the store with the *cockamehmeh* gun? I saw him too.

Cop: What store? What gun?

You: Two blocks back, the big store with the *tsotskehs* in the window.

Cop: Which way did he go?

You: Straight ahead, toward Kishinev.

Cop: You kidding?

You: *Tokke*, am I kidding? Why do you suppose I'm going two miles over the speed limit, ordinarily I drive like an old lady?

Cop: You better not be. (Siren, as he speeds ahead.)

Moral: Never lie to a police officer. If you see a man leave a toy store carrying a junky little thirty-nine-cent gun, tell him so—in no uncertain (Yiddish) terms!

Lesson Two: The Car Salesman

Salesman: [Handing you a pen] All right, sir, that comes to a total of $3,995. If you'll just sign here?

You: I'll sign your *tochas*.

Salesman: My *what*, sir?

You: I'll take the pen and I'll write my name on your *zudik*.

Salesman: I beg your pardon, sir?

You: Yesterday the price was $3,600. I'll pay you the extra $400 when the Pope serves matzo balls for communion.

Salesman: Well, there must have been some misunders . . .

You: *Goniff!* Give me the $3,600 car now and I won't sue General Motors for fifty grand.

Salesman: Well, I'll have to check this with the management.

You: In five minutes the Better Business Bureau, the FBI and the Jewish War Veterans will be here with boards for your show windows.

Salesman: [One minute later] Lucky you, sir. The manager tells me we will be able to give you the car at your price.

You: Good! $3,400 then!

Moral: He who negotiates last negotiates best.

Lesson Three: The Doctor

Doctor: Mr. Harris, why do you phone me at this hour?

You: It's only fifteen minutes past office hours.

Doctor: It's two in the morning, Mr. Harris.

You: Does it matter when a man is croaking?

Doctor: This afternoon you said it was a cold.

You: *Nu?* So it developed.

Doctor: Make an appointment to see me on Thursday.

You: In the funeral home? Tonight I need medication.

Doctor: I'll be the judge of that. See me on Thursday.

You: By Schwartz Drugs they're open all night, you'll make a mercy phone call. A little penicillin, some codeine.

Doctor: Let's both of us just get some sleep now, Mr. Harris.

You: *Veh is mir!* (Cough! Cough!)

Doctor: What is it?

You: You're asking me? Now I know I'm a goner!

Doctor: . . . Mr. Harris . . .

You: Yes, Doctor. A dying man still hopes for last-minute medical discoveries.

Doctor: . . . Mr. Harris, what's the telephone number at Schwartz's?

Moral: An ounce of chutzpah is worth a pound of cure.

At the intermediate level of Verbal Karate the stakes get much bigger—your money, your happiness, your life itself. Proficiency in the following situations will earn you the coveted Gold Lamé Belt.

Lesson Four: Getting a Raise

Boss: Anderson? Yes, you're in the accounting department, aren't you?

You: Right. And during coffee breaks and lunch hours, the only one, sir.

Boss: Let's see, your last increase . . .

You: Just about paid for a *shmateh* my wife is wearing.

Boss: That increase did allow you to move your family, I recall.

You: To the slums, yes, sir.

Boss: Well, your attendance record seems good.

You: Wherever there's heating I go.

Boss: You seem to have been careful about using office supplies.

You: A few of your pencils I sold, that's all.

Boss: Well, Anderson, how does a five-dollar-a-week raise sound to you?

You: Pardon me, sir . . . but how does a pea sound as it falls into the throat of a starving hippopotamus?

Boss: Okay, then. Ten dollars a week, Anderson.

You: Thank you, sir. But I hope you won't refer to me that way again.

Boss: Refer to you what way?

You: As ten-dollars-a-week Anderson. How would it sound to fifteen-dollars-a-week McCarthy and twenty-dollars-a-week Becker?

Moral: Better you should look a gift horse in the mouth than he should look in yours.

Lesson Five: Selling Your Home

Prospect: Frankly, we were looking for something not quite so old.

You: Old? The White House is old . . . the Taj Mahal.

THE POWER OF YIDDISH THINKING

Prospect: Yes, but the crooked walls, the falling plaster . . .

You: You know what they're making the new houses from? *Drek.* In three years they look worse than this.

Prospect: *Drek?* What's this *drek?*

You: It ain't plaster. I know a family just bought a new development house, it fell on them in the middle of the night. Shingles, beams, everything . . . right in their bed.

Prospect: Well, I know the quality of construction isn't what it used to be.

You: For twenty-eight thousand you can't beat this house.

Prospect: But you said the price was thirty-six.

You: And you offered twenty-four.

Prospect: I never said a word.

You: Your eyes told me. Believe me, at twenty-eight thousand they should *shlep* me kicking to the nearest booby hatch.

Prospect: Well . . .

You: You can't patch a little plaster? You can't panel a crooked wall? Why, for twenty-six thousand you're also getting a three-hundred-year-old elm tree, a proven sewage system and quaint community traditions!

Prospect: Did you say twenty-six?

You: Am I frothing at the mouth? Are my eyes rolling in my head? Don't ask questions. Buy before I come to my senses.

Prospect: Well, I guess I can't pass it up at that price.

You: *Gevalt!* Twenty-seven thousand, when my wife hears I'm a dead man.

Prospect: I beg your pardon. We agreed on twenty-six.

You: Okay, tomorrow look for my name in the obituaries. Twenty-six thousand five hundred . . . it's a deal?

Prospect: It's a deal.

Moral: Never bargain in cash or merchandise alone. Few people can resist when you sacrifice yourself in a deal. Chicken soup always tastes better when you throw in a piece of the chicken.

Lesson Six: Saving Your Skin

Mugger: You better stop where you are, daddio. There's twenty-nine of us.

You: I only count twenty-seven. Dropouts! See what you get?

Mugger: Can it, grandpa. Give us your bread and we won't cut you.

You: You want bread, rob a bakery.

Mugger: For a funny man, you sure sweat a lot.

You: You'd sweat too, if you had what I got.

Mugger: What you got?

You: It's not obvious? A man sweats like I do, he's got one thing. The Sweating *Cocka-mehmehs.*

Mugger: Grab his wallet.

You: Touch me and you're good as dead.

Mugger: I think you're putting us on. There ain't no such thing as the sweating whatyousaid.

You: *Machers!* Dropouts! You went to medical school? Go on, try me.

Mugger: If you're so contagious how come they let you in the park?

You: If you're such good boys how come they let you here?

Mugger: Okay, grandpa, get lost. Go sweat somewhere else.

You: Now you're talking. Go rob a leper colony. It's safer.

Mugger #2: Hey, what's a leper colony?

Mugger #1: Dunno. Let's look in the Yellow Pages.

Moral: When a dropout gets the drop in you, drop him with a left and right to the IQ.

Protecting Your Parentage

Probably no better opportunity exists for the Yiddish Upman than in the arena of social bigotry. His centuries-old heritage of pariahhood has given him potent natural defenses against the racial slur and the ethnic insult. The cleverest parlor bigot is no more than a fragile dumpling in the hands of a Yiddish Thinker. Once again, because it is exceptionally apt, let me tell you an old story to illustrate.

Two commuters, from the same suburban town, but strangers, sat next to each other by coincidence every morning. At long last, the one turned to the other and introduced himself.

"Brown's the name," he said, and then spelled it, "B-r-o-w-n. From Boston. And my father, too," he went on, "is named Brown, B-r-o-w-n, and he, too, was born in Boston.

"What's more," he continued, "my grandfather is from Boston and is called Brown, B-r-o-w-n. And," he added, "we are all of us white from head to toe."

At this, the second man smiled courteously and offered his own introduction.

"How do you do," he said. "My name is Cohen. C-ho-haitch-e-n and I vas born in Minsk. And also mine father is named Cohen, C-ho-haitch-e-n, and he too came from Minsk. And mine grandfather too has this name Cohen, C-ho-haitch-e-n, and he came from Pinsk. And," he paused for a sigh, then added, "ve, also, are vhite from head to toe, except for our assholes, which are Brown, B-r-o-w-n!"

You are among strangers at one of those staid suburban cocktail parties. The men are all in brown suits and white shirts. The women flutter about in chiffon serving up rye crisps and library paste. The player piano is bonging out a damaged version of "Tavern in the Town," and the hurricane lamps cast ominous shadows across the painted family photographs. Until now, you have hidden successfully behind a damp martini. You in your black curly mustache, your eight-inch lapels, California suntan and floral socks. All by yourself you are a minority group when suddenly you find yourself staring into a set of solid gray eyeballs. A voice comes with the eyeballs.

Voice: I've been watching you from across the room.

You: Oh, really, gosh, I hadn't noticed.

Voice: I'm Sissy. Sissy Sunderblomsonheusen.

You: Oh, hi.

Voice: You're different from the others here.

You: Am I?

Voice: Aren't you?

You: Uh . . .

Voice: I've never seen you at church.

You: Well, heh heh, you know what they say, "Right church, wrong pew."

Voice: They're all Episcopal Evangelical Brethren of the Ascension here. And you?

You: Me? Oh, just a sinner, I guess.

Voice: I bet you didn't work for Goldwater.
You: Oh, yes. I mean, no, that's right.
Voice: It's okay. You're a . . . "democrat," aren't you?
You: Yes, as a matter of fact, I am.
Voice: You see? I knew you were different.
You: Well, now that's settled.
Voice: Greek? Italian? Your parents, I mean.
You: Look here, Miss uh . . .
Voice: Sissy. Oh, everybody knows Sissy. Song leader at the White Citizens Council. I know the words to the "Horst Wessel," everything . . .
You: Sure. Well, Miss Sissy, if you really want to know about my parents. Daddy, you see, was black.
Voice: Black.
You: Black. And queer.
Voice: Q . . . ?
You: And mums . . . mums was a Polish army camp follower! And now, if you'll forgive me, I'm going out to find a small American boy and eat his head.

One-upping the One-upman

I stated earlier that in form and style Yiddish Upmanship cannot compete with the finely honed tactics of the gentlemen disciples of Stephen Potter. One is, after all, a game, the other a war. The Yiddish Thinker has no use for games. It is only when they get out of hand that he enters, and then, with chilling effect.

It is your high school reunion. After twenty years, like most of the other men present, you've lost some hair, put on some weight, made a few dollars but haven't set the world on fire. So what are you hearing?

Fred: Wholesale jewelry. I tell you, it turned me around. Now I'm in nine cities with thirty-six units.

Made the first million on ten per cent markups.
Eugene?

Eugene: Me? Built up my credit ten years, socked fifty
grand into developments, skimmed off the profits
and got a bank chair. Christ, I practically own
Cincinnati. Harold?

Harold: Commodities exchange. Waited for my chance
and got a bargain seat, six thou. Made a hundred grand plus swing the first week, netted
half a mil in two years, took it out and threw it
all into franchise franchising. Good chance now
to be the first franchiser of franchise franchisers.
Sam? Sam? All faces turn to you. "Sam, what did
you finally wind up in?

And you see this is not a game, but a war, and you say:
Garbage. I'm a garbage man.

At the most advanced level of Verbal Karate nobody wins.
The best you can hope for is a Mexican—or should we say
Jewish—standoff. For at this grade you will be playing the
game with the people who invented it, and in their court.
On the other hand, if you handle it with skill you'll score
many more points than you ever did before, and you'll have
a lot of fun doing it.

Proficiency at this topmost level will entitle you to an honor
few Gentiles and not very many Jews can claim—the rare
and prestigious Borscht Belt!

The Jewish Restaurant

From city to city, the decor may change a bit, the menu
selections may vary in name, if not content, but one thing
remains pretty much the same in Jewish restaurants the

world over: the attitude of the management, particularly the waiters.

An unassuming Gentile, wandering into a Jewish restaurant, may at first be put off, then unnerved by the Jewish waiter. Next time you enter a Ratner's or an Ashkenaz (countermen) try a little Yiddish Upmanship. It could turn out quite differently.

You: Waiter, is this table free?

Waiter: No, it's five hundred dollars.

You: I ask because it's got *shmutz* all over it.

Waiter: Can I help it? Pigs eat here. [He gives a quick once-over with a towel snap, flicking a few crumbs off the seat, and runs.]

You: [Yelling to him five tables away.] I'm ordering!

Waiter: Don't holler. I wouldn't forget your face. [He returns, pencil poised. He is preoccupied with something far across the room.] *Nu?* What do you want?

You: What is the Barbra Streisand Special?

Waiter: You don't want it!

You: How do you know what I don't want? [He is still not looking at you.]

Waiter: I'm only here thirty years, I don't know what's good?

You: If it's no good, why is it on the *verkockteh* menu?

Waiter: Am I the owner? The Barbra Streisand is poison. Today, the cabbage soup.

You: I hate cabbage soup.

Waiter: Then the *kishke farfel* plate.

You: It's fattening.

Waiter: You need it.

You: How can you tell? You still haven't looked at me. [Suddenly he regards you. He is no longer a busy waiter, but a worried, solicitous auntie.]

Waiter: Mister? How long since you ate anything? You know I can see your ribs through your Brooks Brothers?

You: So you're giving me *kishke?* You want I should look like you with my *boich* six inches in front of my belt buckle?

Waiter: You're right. In this day and age a successful person should eat only olives and celery. Are you a Yale man?

You: What's with the *shmei drei?* I thought you were so busy with customers.

Waiter: Let them all *pager.* Tell me more about yourself, it's not so often that I get such an educated clientele.

You: Just bring me a corned beef sandwich.

Waiter: Whatever you want, *tataleh.*

You: And, waiter . . . make it *lean!*

Waiter: [From across the room] If there's even one ounce of fat after thirty years let them hang me by the *gorgul* with the salamis! [Later the sandwich comes, and it's fat and so what. You had a good time.]

The Resort Vacation

It must have happened to everybody once. You made your reservations and paid your deposit far in advance for "two glorious weeks at Wisconsin's Most Elegant Resort." Or maybe it was "Nevada's Most Fabulous," or "Mississippi's Most Luxurious." When at last you arrived, however, you might as well have dropped in from the moon, for all the management knew about it. And what did you do? You probably accepted what was available and swore you'd never go to such a place again. If you'll forgive my saying so, that was very Gentile of you. The following scene is set somewhere in that well-known Jewish Shangri-la called the Catskills. However, it might just as well be Gentile Gardens, Georgia, or WASP Acres, Washington.

Reservations Clerk: You say that you are not satisfied with your accommodations, sir?

You: *Shtoonk!* I wanted the Main Lodge and you give me Abraham Lincoln's boyhood home.

Clerk: How long ago did you make the reservation, sir?

You: Ten years ago last *Donnershtick,* what does it matter?

Clerk: I'm afraid the Main Lodge is full, sir.

You: What does a *lemishkeh* know? Give me the manager.

Manager: What is the trouble, sir?

You: The trouble is I've got three kids and a wife freezing their *tochases* off in Abraham Lincoln's outhouse.

Manager: But The Illini is one of our most commodious cottages, sir.

You: For who, am I Kit Carson? Is my wife wearing coonskin? I ordered Main Lodge, you'll give me Main Lodge.

Manager: Well, there is one suite in the Main Lodge, sir, but I'm afraid you'll have to share a bath.

You: *Chob dir in bod!* From toilet seat germs we can die in the city. For this we don't need to come to the mountains. I'll see the owner.

Owner: I'm Mr. Horwitz. What can I do for you?

You: Horwitz, you the *shamus* here?

Owner: I am.

You: Do I look like a relative of Daniel Boone?

Owner: No.

You: Would you put your family's *zudiks* on a public toilet while who knows what *verkockteh* people are also using it?

Owner: I wouldn't.

You: Will you give me a suite in the Main Lodge that I wouldn't have to drive back a hundred miles tonight and report at Horwitz's there is *shmutz* in the swimming pool, *siff* in the beds and *chazerai* for dinner?

Owner: Sir, for a gentleman like yourself there is always room in the Main Lodge at Horwitz's.

Marrying into a Jewish Family

A few decades ago, this section would not have been necessary. But the fact is today that more and more Jewish boys and girls are marrying non-Jews, or vice versa. Both partners, in such marriages, may face certain psychological adjustments. For our purposes, however, let us examine what special preparation might be helpful to the new Gentile in-law who must confront a large, chummy and razor-tongued Jewish family. Bride and groom, shy or bold, this is the one arena where a little Yiddish Upmanship could win the day.

It is your first holiday dinner at the home of your new

in-laws. You have just blown the dust off the family bourbon bottle. Bracing for the evening ahead, you pour yourself a double, when from behind a steaming brisket you hear your mother-in-law's voice say, "Oy, darling . . . one sip of that and I'd be *shikker*." You belt the sinful liquid down and, then, catching her eye through a space in the mountain of gefilte fish, say, "Ah, Mom, but you haven't lived until you've been *verfnyifkit!*"

Across the table from you, grandma, whiskery and inscrutable, has fixed her attention upon your tastefully Clairoled scalp. At long last she utters malevolently, "This is your natural hair color, this blond?" You fire back, "No, grandma, it's a wig. Actually, I've been *parech* since the age of thirteen."

Fat Uncle Irving is in a generous mood. Igniting an expensive panatela, he allows as how he once almost married a Gentile girl. "Almost, Uncle?" It is your turn to say, "What a nice *mitzvah* for the girl."

Second Cousin Bertha, who has a "Catholic friend at the office" and, hence, is a self-proclaimed Knower of Gentiles and intimate of the non-Jewish world, inquires about your parentage. "What was your maiden name again?" she asks, "McKay? McKee?"

"McKaplan!"

Finally, just about the time of the third dessert course, the discussion turns, inevitably, to the subject of offspring. Someone—a grandfather, an aunt, perhaps—causes all cherry-cheesecake-eating to stop with an inquiry such as: "And what will you name the children if they're boys?"

Allow the import of this question to take hold of your audience for a moment. Then, in grim earnest, announce, "Well, we were thinking of either Luke, Matthew and Xavier [Pause here. Ever see eyebrows raised to the hairline level?] . . . or else Maish, Izzie and Haskellazar!"

These few examples should be sufficient to give you the idea. If you are already married but haven't exactly been the hit of the Cousin's Club, just wait for your openings and then show 'em your Verbal Karate. The more it stings, the more they'll love you for it.

"There is a purifying power in laughter—both for individuals and for nations. If they have a sense of humor, they have the key—to good sense, to simple thinking, to a peaceable temper, and to a cultured outlook on the world."—Lin Yutang (Yiddish)

11

GEOPOLITICAL YIDDISH
or
A Plan for World Niceness

Should Red China be admitted to the UN? Should the Russians be forced to pay up? Is World War III inevitable? These questions send seasoned diplomats running to the rest room to throw up. Ordinary people turn pale and change the subject to baby-sitters or color TV. Is it possible that Yiddish and Yiddish Thinking hold the answers to such earthshaking problems? Though harsh and cantankerous with words, Yiddish cynicism is, after all, good-natured cynicism. It never expects too much of the world. It values reasonableness over reason. It is in favor of peace, but understands peacefulness better. The Yiddish Thinker could be the best of all possible diplomats, for he hardly ever means what he says, yet always seems to say what he means. He curses when he means to love, he compliments in order to criticize.

Suppose that every statesman in the world today had spent

ten years of his life with a Jewish family in New Jersey, or worked summers as a boy in the Catskills. Or in some way or other had the opportunity to develop a Yiddish point of view. How much differently would future biographers record recent world events? Perhaps something like this:

The Australian's mouth was going on and on about tariffs, and Lou Wong, the UN delegate from Nationalist China, admired a snapshot of his grandchildren playing water polo at Grossinger's of the Himalayas. He had ordered out for Jewish food the night before and, finding himself without any Alka-Seltzer, couldn't sleep a wink. So he spent the long hours thinking about his relatives on the Red Mainland. Would he ever see them again, the poor *shlemazels?* Slogans they get. Who can eat slogans? The only answer was to get Red China into the UN. But how? His own government, big *machers,* wouldn't hear of a two-China policy. And with all their troubles neither would the Reds. Yet anybody with any brains wanted Red China in the UN. Even the Americans, those *lemmels,* would rather face the Reds in the UN cafeteria than in Manchuria. By five in the morning, when the heartburn finally passed, Lou had devised a plan which he felt could not fail.

In the corridor, after the session, Lou bumped into the U.S. ambassador. "Bushkin," he said, "next week I'm putting up Red China for admission."

"You?" Bushkin laughed. "They'll make moo goo gai pan out of you in Taiwan. Anyhow, you know the Reds won't sit still for two Chinas. And *we* don't even like the idea of one China."

"I'm not suggesting two Chinas. It will be *three* Chinas."

The American scoffed. "You crazy? What's the *shtick?*"

Lou bit off the end of a fat, green, black-market Cuban cigar. "Look, I talked with Communists last week. They don't believe this hard-line *drek* anymore. All they want is good steak and a shower, and maybe some eleven-bedroom tract homes."

Bushkin nodded. He wondered privately what it would take to pick up a little suburban real estate around Peking. "Okay," he said, "but what do you mean, *three* Chinas?"

"Don't be a *shmegehgeh*." The oriental shook his head. "One, Nationalist China. Two, Communist China. Three . . . *Cockamehmeh* China. Out of eight hundred million Chinese there's maybe twenty real Communists and ten Nationalists. The rest are *cockamehmeh* Chinamen."

"But your people are always worried about saving face," Bushkin said.

"Face shmace!" Lou retorted. "They'd rather have a good steak!"

Meanwhile, in another corner of the UN building, Nick the Russian was haranguing Nevilleh, the Englishman. "Dues? For your imperialist wars, from us you'll get *cerebronis!*"

Nevilleh glared at the man who only recently had guided him through the Kremlin's underground Stock Exchange. "*Momser*," he hollered, "with the money you're saving in the Far East you could buy a warm sweater for everybody in Asia."

Nick frowned. "Asia is now your worry," he said. "Talk to your *lantzmen,* the Americans, about money." He flicked on his two-way wrist radio made in Japan by American exchange students, and swore. "*Goniff!* U. S. Cyanamid is going up four points this minute, and you're keeping me here with this dues *nahrishkeit*."

Nevilleh quickly produced a check made out for fifty million rubles to the UN treasury. "You'll sign," he said, "because if you don't, I'll tell the Africans you can't afford."

"What we can't afford? We're on the moon already almost. Everybody has a nice car. Who will believe we can't afford?"

The Englishman smiled, picking his teeth with a solid gold,

sickle-shaped swizzle stick, purchased by his wife at Nina Khrushchev's garage sale. "Is it true that the caviar at Kremlin receptions is now being diluted with poppy seeds?"

"Feh!" the Russian spat. "Who believes such lies?"

The Englishman persisted. "Is it not true," he went on, "that Russian forests are so depleted you are importing Polish toilet paper?"

"*Gevalt!* Who says so?" the Russian sputtered.

Now the Englishman had him eyeball to eyeball. "Do you deny," he said, "the Soviet treasury is so poor that just last month all the memorabilia of the Revolution were pawned with a man named Futterman in the Bronx?"

"I'm *pagering*," the Russian croaked. Nevertheless, he slipped the check into a fat roll of Swiss bank notes and, rushing to the street, hailed a Wall Street-bound cab.

Meanwhile, in a Parisian park, a trio of men played gin rummy and took a little sun. Kibbitz-Lodge, the baggy American, and the well-laundered Pompleman, French and immaculate in his sleeveless undershirt, silently snapped the cards. Fidelkeh, the Cuban, kept score.

"Gin!" said the American, spreading his hand, and then admiring a passing mademoiselle—"Pompleman, if I was as snooty-tooty as you are, we would have had World War III a long time ago already."

"Give the *goniff* thirty-two." Pompleman indicated where Fidelkeh should put the score. "Look who's snooty-tootying," he went on, shuffling a new deck. "What is this *mishegas* you've got going in the Far East? If it's not a war, are you playing *pisha paysha?*"

Kibbitz-Lodge slowly peeled the cards and, shaking his head, clucked, "*Nu nu.* You think us Americans enjoy all this fighting and carrying on? We're a *haymisheh* people. We love kiddies and baseball games. What do we know from jungles and rice paddies?"

"So get out of there already!" the swarthy man in the khaki underwear finally spoke up.

"*Mishugeneh!*" the American turned on him. "You and your *verkockteh* revolutions. It's ten years by you already and nobody's even getting *farfel* on Christmas."

"You wait," said Fidelkeh, "next year we'll get."

"*Ahftseloches* you'll get."

The Frenchman rose, rearranged his tricolored suspenders, and yawned. "*Genug shoen*" he said. "Enough bombs. Enough wars. From now on we have only Niceness."

"Niceness? How only Niceness?" Kibbitz-Lodge asked.

"Listen," said Pompleman, "next week we'll play by his place." He motioned toward the Cuban. "But instead of our usual game, we'll throw a regular Las Vegas, with gambling and drinking and tootsies . . ."

"Tootsies even!" Kibbitz-Lodge looked worried.

"The works," said Pompleman. "And everybody we know who has a bomb, we'll invite."

Fidelkeh put the Kem cards away. "Well, I don't get it," he said, "and how will tootsies bring Niceness."

Kibbitz-Lodge was clucking once more. "*Nu nu nu,*" he said, "and whose wife when she heard about it would ever let him in the house again?"

An uneasy silence followed. Finally it was Pompleman who spoke.

"My thinking exactly," he sighed. "My plan is based on an old French saying I just made up." He pinched his skin to check the day's accumulation of suntan, and winked. "A fella whose wife won't even let him in the door ain't in no position to start a war!"

Epilogue

The following week, in a long session that brought much kissing, tears and discussion on the best way to prepare a good steak, the UN unanimously welcomed both Communist China and *Cockamehmeh* China into the Brotherhood of Nations. Russia paid its dues with a little bit extra. And in Havana, after a wild night of daiquiris, tootsies and gin rummy . . . Niceness descended upon the world.

Test Your YQ

The time has come in your education when it is vital to have some measurement of your progress. Few foreign languages require you to think in them before you learn to speak them. Yiddish is the exception. So now, submit yourself to the first test ever devised to determine your YQ, or Yiddish Quotient. Give yourself two points for each correct answer. A YQ of 100 is perfect. Eighty is nice. Sixty is eh. And anything below fifty, I think you're reading the wrong book. Answers appear at the end of the test.

THE BIG PUTDOWN
Multiple choice, circle one.

1. The lady at your door is collecting for Arthritis, and won't believe you when you say you're broke. Do you:
   A) tell her you don't support Greek charities?
   B) hit her with a crutch?
   C) write a check for a nickel?

2. Six months after the wedding your daughter has a baby. Do you:
   A) beat up your son-in-law?
   B) claim she was secretly married three months earlier?
   C) say: "If it'll make you feel better, we'll ask her to take twelve months with the next one"?

3. A neighbor points out all the crabgrass in your lawn.
   Do you:
   A) claim that even a weed has a right to live?
   B) smack him in the mouth?
   C) lie that you're planning to resod the whole lawn next
      week?

4. You are at a cocktail party, and a bore is dropping the
   names of famous people he knows up to and including
   the President. Do you:
   A) listen politely?
   B) say: "If you run into Pat, would you tell her she can
      afford to eat some pies, milk shakes, it might soften
      up that snake puss of hers"?
   C) spill your drink on his tie?

5. Your teenage son wears flowers in his beard and spends
   his time at love-ins. Do you:
   A) send him to a psychiatrist?
   B) water his beard?
   C) offer to set him up in the florist business?

6. A neighbor shows you around the new $20,000 addition
   to his house, ticking off every expense including tax.
   Do you:
   A) ask him if he heard about the shopping center going
      up across the street?
   B) compliment his good taste?
   C) trip him going down the stairs?

7. A business colleague buys ten new suits on his lunch
   hour. The suit you're wearing is so old it glows in the
   dark. Do you:
   A) explain: "A man who's retiring to Palm Beach doesn't
      need a lot of business suits"?
   B) complain that the stores never carry your size?
   C) turn so that the glare of your seat doesn't hit him in
      the eyes?

8. The doctor tells you to stop smoking. Do you:
    A) promise to follow his advice?
    B) light up and say, "You could be right"?
    C) explain that if you quit smoking you'll only gain weight, drop dead of a heart attack, and for this kind of advice who needs a doctor?

9. The plumber tells you that to fix a leaky toilet you must replace the whole plumbing system. Do you:
    A) call in another plumber?
    B) smack him in the mouth?
    C) ask him if he knows his head is leaking?

10. The hypnotist has just stretched your wife between two chairs and is standing on her stomach. Do you:
    A) applaud?
    B) tell him, "Big deal, with her girdle on I could do the same thing"?
    C) request that he jump up and down?

THE FLAT STATEMENT (CHUTZPAH)

Are these glittering generalities true or false according to Yiddish Thinking?

11. All children must attend summer camp.
12. Color TV stinks.
13. Doris Day is a sweetheart.
14. Diet cola tastes better than the real thing.
15. Nobody can understand English movies.
16. Compact cars are sensible.
17. Las Vegas is a city of sin.
18. Short, skinny children are all anemic.
19. There is no such thing as a natural blonde.
20. Harvard is overrated.

THE QUESTION/ANSWER

Place the letter of the appropriate answer after the numbered question.

21. Can you play poker to-night with the boys? (   )
22. How do you like this new jet airplane? (   )
23. Is it cold enough for you? (   )
24. Do you think there's life on other planets? (   )
25. Can't you quit smoking? (   )
26. How much longer till we get to Grandma's? (   )
27. Would you care for some smoked oysters? (   )
28. Was this your first heart attack? (   )
29. How do you want to pay for this TV repair job, cash or charge? (   )
30. Do you promise to tell the truth and nothing but the truth? (   )

(A) Have I ever been west of Jersey that I know who is living there?
(B) Can a fish climb a tree?
(C) Why don't you offer me a human hand on toast?
(D) Would I say I don't like it and get it mad at me?
(E) Should I stick my head in a snowbank?
(F) If it was my last would I be here to talk about it?
(G) Do you promise to be-lieve me if I do?
(H) Is my wife drugged and locked in the closet?
(I) If I say two days will you shut up for an hour?
(J) When you're throwing money in a sewer, does it matter how?

THE YIDDISH-GOYISH VALUE GAP

After each item in the following pairs, put a Y if you think it is Yiddish, or a G if Goyish.

31. Apples   Melons
32. Hospital rooms   U. S. Space Program

33. Barry Goldwater   Sidney Poitier
34. Kibbutzes   Health spas
35. Nova Scotia   Nova Scotia salmon
36. Pinochle   Motorcycles
37. Scotch and water   Frozen daiquiris
38. Doctors   Nurses
39. Stereo   Outdoor concerts
40. Pork roast   Bacon

Match up these famous people with their shticks.

41. Kirk Douglas ( )
42. Ann Landers ( )
43. Eldridge Cleaver ( )
44. Billy Graham ( )
45. Arthur Godfrey ( )
46. Charles de Gaulle ( )
47. Grace Kelly ( )
48. Ralph Nader ( )
49. Hugh Hefner ( )
50. William F. Buckley ( )

(A) He's scared stiff of cars.
(B) He knew exactly what to do, you couldn't even make a suggestion.
(C) An American who speaks with a foreign accent.
(D) He can't stand white people, even for a minute.
(E) A chin made him rich.
(F) She waves a lot from balconies and airplanes.
(G) He likes to pray outside.
(H) He uses words so long it hurts his face to say them.
(I) She knows what's good for you, she doesn't have to meet you.
(J) He thinks sex is clean.

ANSWERS

1.C. 2.C. 3.A. 4.B. 5.C. 6.A. 7.A. 8.C. 9.C. 10.B.

11. True. Only summer camp develops independence, responsibility and a healthy complexion. Without it, kids would be helpless, skin-diseased loafers.

12. False. Color TV is the most fabulous thing to come along since plastic furniture covers.

13. True. She's so adorable you could pinch her little bottom. And with her sexy pictures it almost makes you forget your hysterectomy.

14. True. Diet cola is a miracle of medical science. The greatest thing since color TV.

15. True. The way the English speak English, a person can't even enjoy a box popcorn without losing the plot.

16. False. Compact cars are tinny with hard seats, you could get killed for a few pennies you save on gasoline.

17. False. Las Vegas is gorgeous. It's the greatest thing to happen in America since diet cola.

18. True. Such children should be taken five times a week to the pediatrician, makes no difference if their parents are four foot nine.

19. True. You're not fooling anybody, honey. Even in Sweden they're all dyed.

20. True. Harvard Shmarvard. A little more grass, a little more ivy, and you learn to pick your nose with your little finger sticking out.

21.(H) 22.(D) 23.(E) 24.(A) 25.(B) 26.(I) 27.(C) 28.(F) 29.(J) 30.(G)

31.GY 32.YG 33.GY 34.GY 35.GY 36.YG 37.GY 38.YG 39.YG 40.GY

41.(E) 42.(I) 43.(D) 44.(G) 45.(C) 46.(B) 47.(F) 48.(A) 49.(J) 50.(H)

GLOSSARY

*Ahftseloches (Ahf tseh *law* chus): What's coming to you. And it's all bad.

Bakockt (Bah *kockt*): All crapped up.

Betgevante (*Bet* geh vahn teh): A nonsense word for cheap.

Boich (Boych): The belly. Especially the paunchy kind.

Boobeleh (*Boo* beh leh): Darling.

Cerebronis (Seh reh *braw* niss): Fly specks.

Chalyicher (*Chahl* yih cher): A cripple.

Chazerai (Chah zuh *rye*): Junky, unnutritious food.

Chob dir in bod (Chawb dir in *buhd*): A threat. "I'll get you in the bathtub."

Chutzpah (*Chuts* pah): Colossal nerve.

Cockamehmeh (*Kah* kuh may meh): Foolish; junky; ill-conceived.

Donnershtick (*Dun* ner shtick): Thursday.

Drek (Dreck): Crap.

**Gefilte fish (Geh *fill* teh fish):

Fish balls.

Gehockteh flaish (Geh *hock* teh *flaysh*): Minced meat.

Genug shoen (Geh *nook* shane): "Enough already!"

Gevalt (Geh *vahlt*): "Heaven help us!"

Goniff (*Gah* niff): A thief.

Gorgul (*Gore* gul): The throat.

Haymisheh (*Hay* mis sheh): Homey. Especially that type of person.

Kishinev (*Kish* nev): A remote place.

Kishke farfel plate (*Kish* key *far* ful): A combination dinner of stuffed derma and something like minced noodles made of matzo meal.

Kockers (*cock* erz): Shitters.

Lantzmen (*lahnts* men): Countrymen.

Lemishkeh (*leh* mish keh): A wishy-washy person.

Lemmels (*leh* mulz): Nincompoops.

Machers (*Mah* cherz): Big shots.

Matzo balls (*Mott* suh): Dumplings of matzo meal.

Megilla (Muh *gil* luh): A huge

* The letters *ch* are pronounced as in Scottish word "loch" or German "Ach."
** G's are hard, as in "giggle."

scroll containing the Jewish law.

Misha mishina (*Mih* shuh mih *shee* neh): A nonsense word for cheap.

Mishegas (Mish shuh *gahs*): A craziness.

Mishugeneh (Mih *shuh* geh neh): A crazy person.

Mitzvah (*Mitts* vuh): A blessing.

Momser (*Mom* zer): A bastard.

Nahrishkeit (*Nah* rish kite): Nonsense.

Nu (noo): So? What then? So What!

Nudniks (*nood* nicks): Pests.

Pager (*pay* gur): To die.

Parech (parch): Bald.

Pipik (*pih* pick): Bellybutton.

Pisha paysha (*Pih* shuh *pay* shuh): A child's card game.

Rachmonis (Rahch *maw* nis): Pity.

Sechel (*Seh* chul): Wits; intelligence; shrewdness.

Shadchen (*Shod* chen): Marriage broker.

Shamus (*shah* mus): Anybody who is in charge.

Shikker (*shik* ker): Drunk.

Shlemazels: (Shluh *mah* zulz): Unlucky fools.

Shlemiel (Shluh *meal*): A fool.

Shlep (Shlep): To drag.

Shmateh (*Shmah* teh): A rag.

Shmegehgeh (Shmuh *geh* gee): A dope.

Shmei drei (*Shmy* dry): Baloney; hot air.

Shmuck (Shmuck): A very bad word for a fool.

Shmutz (shmuts): Filth.

Shnoogle (*Shnoo* gul): Cuddle.

Shnorer (*Shnaw* rer): Freeloader.

Shtick (shtick): Literally, a piece. A person's specialty; a gimmick.

Shtoonk (Shtoonk): A stinker.

Tataleh (*Tah* tah leh): Literally, little father. A term of endearment.

Tochas (*Taw* chus): The hind end.

Tokke (*Tah* key): "Would you believe?"

Tsotskeh (*Tsots* key): A bauble. A cheap little thing.

Tzimmis (*Tsih* miss): A vegetable stew.

Veh is mir (*Vah* is mir): "Woe is me!"

Vehr geharget (*Vehr* geh *har* get): "Drop dead!"

Verfnyifkit (Fur *fnyif* kit): Yentehs (*Yen* tehs): Busybodies.
Dead drunk.

Verkockteh (Fur *kock* teh): Zudik (*Zoo* dick): The hind
Worse than crappy.   end.